THE PARTICULARS OF PETER

THE PARTICULARS OF PETER

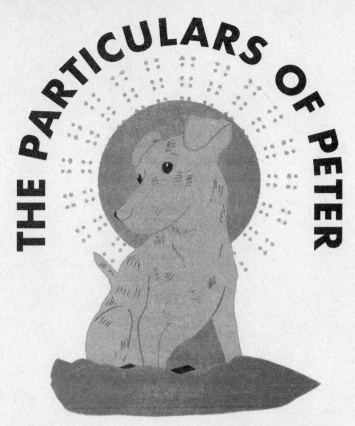

Dance Lessons, DNA Tests, and Other Excuses to Hang Out with My Perfect Dog

KELLY CONABOY

GRAND
CENTRAL
PUBLISHING

New York Boston

Grand Central Publishing
Hachette Book Group
1290 Avenue of the Americas, New York, NY 10104
grandcentralpublishing.com
twitter.com/grandcentralpub

First Edition: December 2020

Grand Central Publishing is a division of Hachette Book Group, Inc. The Grand Central Publishing name and logo is a trademark of Hachette Book Group, Inc.

The publisher is not responsible for websites (or their content) that are not owned by the publisher.

The Hachette Speakers Bureau provides a wide range of authors for speaking events. To find out more, go to www.hachettespeakersbureau.com or call (866) 376-6591.

Print book interior design by Marie Mundaca

"What Is My dog?" was originally published by the Outline. "Dogs Should Be Able to Talk for 25 Minutes Per Day" was originally published by the Hairpin. Portions of "Should I Spy on My Dog?" were originally published by *New York Magazine* under the title "The Case for Buying a Doggy Spy Cam (If You Really Need One)."

Library of Congress Cataloging-in-Publication Data
Names: Conaboy, Kelly, author.
Title: The particulars of Peter : dance lessons, DNA tests, and other excuses to hang out with my perfect dog / Kelly Conaboy.
Description: First edition. | New York : Grand Central Publishing, 2020. |
Identifiers: LCCN 2020030166 | ISBN 9781538717868 (hardcover) | ISBN 9781538717851 (ebook)
Subjects: LCSH: Conaboy, Kelly. | Dog owners--United States--Biography. | Human-animal relationships. | Dog adoption.
Classification: LCC SF422.82.C66 A3 2020 | DDC 636.70092/9--dc23
LC record available at https://lccn.loc.gov/2020030166

ISBNs: 978-1-5387-1786-8 (hardcover), 978-1-5387-1785-1 (ebook)

Printed in the United States of America

LSC-H

Printing 1, 2020

For Mom, Dad, and Peter

CONTENTS

Contents

PREFACE

I need to start by acknowledging some guilt I have about all of this. I've spent the majority of my writing career not writing anything particularly personal, because I'm shy and private and the idea of selling my privacy creeped me out, but also because I didn't particularly have anything I wanted to say about myself. (I don't have any delusions, though, that I ever attempted to not be the story. Journalists will rightly gripe when a writer turns a piece about something or someone else into a piece about themselves, and I'll always join in on the griping, because I love a good gripe, but most often when I write about something or someone else, what I want you to notice most are the clever asides; the funny way of phrasing things. Yes, we're happy to be taken on this journey about why cinnamon sticks are more expensive than ground cinnamon, but mostly what we like is this charming writer.)

I was also, and maybe still am, pretty sure that in order to write about your life in a funny and compelling way you have to lie, or at least stretch the truth, to make your story seem worth telling; more vibrant and memorable than anyone's life actually is. I don't like the idea of doing this, even though I do like reading it. This is mostly because I fear even the lies about my life wouldn't be particularly funny or compelling.

But then I adopted Peter. I want to acknowledge, too, that it's very difficult to figure out the vocabulary around the "ownership" of a dog. I know I don't own him, other than legally. "Dog owner" feels cruel, and it's not something I like to identify as, but it is unfortunately the clearest term, and one I use a few times within the book. Dog guardian, human companion, "dog mom"... I think they're all sort of distracting in their too-obvious attempts to be something other than the one we all know, which is "dog owner." I admit that this sucks, and I'm sorry. And while we're on the topic of language, as far as a pronoun goes, in this book I usually use "he" to refer to the general dog, because the dog I know best—the subject of this book—is biologically male. I hate to give men more visibility than they already have, but that's the way it is. I do, however, know dogs can also be girls.

Anyway, after I adopted Peter he became all I wanted to write about. He replaced anything I previously found curious, and anything I was previously interested in. He is my great love and my obsession. My sweet number one man. And you can write about your dog while keeping readers at a distance, to an extent. I wrote about attempting to build a gingerbread house that he could fit inside of; I wrote about how to respond to someone on the street when they pay him a compliment. But what I really wanted to write about was him. Everything about who he is as a dog is interesting to me.

But this proved difficult. Although he is his own being, he is my companion animal, and because we are of different species, and because I am not an expert in dog cognition, the majority of what I know about him is in relation to me. I feel like I do know him deeply, but of course I only know him through the eyes of a human, and I can, for the most part, only talk about him that way. I know how he is when we're together. I know how I am, and how I've changed, in relation to and because of him. I don't think he could be portrayed honestly, the way that I know him, without including bits of myself as part of the story. And I really, really want him to be seen, because I think he is truly special. (Just like your dog is, I'm sure, if you have one.) (If you don't have one—why?) This is not the guilt-ridden part, though, this is just the embarrassing part—that I have to be here, too.

The guilt-ridden part is that I am doing this for money. I'm a writer and I love writing, and I love thinking and writing about Peter in particular, but I am getting paid to do this. It's an odd thing about the dog memoir genre. We are ostensibly the ones who love our dogs so much that we are compelled to write thousands and thousands of words about them, but we're also the ones, it can be said, who are not satisfied keeping their dogs as what they are: dogs. We turn them into public figures, into content. Worse, we use them as a vehicle to think and write about ourselves. We use them for a paycheck or at least the hope of one. We turn them into work.

Here is something that worries me: I'm judgmental about people who use their dogs as fame-grabbing or moneymaking tools on social media. Particularly those who run accounts in the "voice" of their dogs, the voice usually being something embarrassing like, "ooh me mommy she luff to give me yummy good scarfums!"—like, why do you think your dog talks like that? Jesus. It's hard not to see the dogs being used as a prop in these sort of accounts. An often anthropomorphized version of what a dog is. A means to an end. A tool only for human gain, and not even particularly worthwhile human gain: clicks, followers, favs.

But is what I'm doing now that far removed? I'm hoping you're thinking *of course*, but as I write this alone I'm not sure. Peter isn't getting much out of this. Mostly I tried not to bother him with it, and otherwise I tried to give him some fun experiences. He took agility classes, he went to a dog festival. But even in these cases—I'm so sorry to take you down all of these horrible paths of self-obsession, please feel free to skip ahead—it's guilt-making to be a writer when undergoing experiences. I always hate admitting that I'm doing something to write about it to those who are doing it simply for the experience of doing it. It makes people suspicious, like I might have some sort of cruel ulterior motive, and it makes me feel like a phony. It's better if you can refrain from divulging your writerly intentions, but then you feel like a liar, and I've found that it always eventually comes out anyway.

And this is bad enough when it's just me. But to have Peter alongside me, it opens up the opportunity for the understandable thought that not only are my motives as a person incorrect, but so are my motives as a dog, um, guardian. That I'm using him as a prop, as a vehicle for my work. *She is dragging around a dog for her own means. Her intentions are not altruistic!*

But I think he deserves to be documented and remembered, by someone better than me, in fact, but unfortunately I'm the writer who has him, so I'm his best shot. I want to know everything I can about him. And I want you to get a sense of him. And more than anything else, I wanted an excuse to hang out with him all the time, and think about him all the time, and write about him all the time. I wanted to spend time getting to know him. I feel so lucky that I was able to do that, to make him into work. What an incredible scam.

THE PARTICULARS OF PETER

Chapter 1

HOW DID WE GET HERE?

What did I do before Peter? I'm trying to remember. I have to imagine there were things. I did computer, I guess. Typed. Sat alone. Shuffled around the apartment in stockinged feet. Made dinner and ate it while doing, what? Looking at the wall? And who did I feed a noodle to? No one?

It's almost too gruesome to recall.

I think once a person has a dog the idea of not having one quickly becomes absurd. I know there are other ways a person can fill their time—golf, et cetera. I know you can Hula-Hoop. You can pan for gold, or "do some work at a café." I know a person can exist without the ability to make a creature they love thrash with uncontrollable joy, wild-eyed and ecstatic, at the mere mention of din—; hush, that's enough, they're already excited. I know you can watch TV without a dog resting his paws and head on your leg, breathing quietly, warming you and allowing you to feel like you're having a *real human experience* rather than idly ingesting *The Sopranos*. I know you can go to sleep without a dog in your bed and wake up without a little face staring down at you, whiskers in your eyes, and a nose dripping onto your skin, waiting for you to take him outside so that he might urinate. But... why? Why even wake up at all?

If I'm being honest, though, the idea that you're going to have to take the dog outside to urinate (et cetera) a few times every day for the rest of his life is something that *also* quickly becomes absurd. You wake up and think, *again*? Not that it's gross, it's not, but the completely altered routine, the to-dos you don't even get to add to your to-do list because it would be like adding "digest" or "breathe"—it's odd. The strange newness of this fades after about two months, in my experience. Then the routine becomes unremarkable, the only experience of novelty now being the dog's, again and again, in realizing that—against all odds—if you can even believe it for a single second—I promise you this is not a drill—they are getting the opportunity to take: another walk.

I guess another principal absurdity is the fact that anyone entrusted you with a dog at all. (I assume all of these feelings are amplified with human children, but I don't know about that firsthand, my apologies; I only know about Peter, who is a dog.) Even if you had to jump through hoops to get your dog—apartment visits, letters of recommendation, several emails begging the dog rescue to let you adopt your foster dog even though you know it's against their rules—it's eventually just you and your dog in a room and you look at him and think, *Oh my god. What do I do with you now?*

Going over the series of unplanned events that led to something good always makes me feel tense. I'd rather not think about how easily something could not have been. It's true in this case particularly (the case of how I ended up with Peter), because I was very close to not being able to keep him at all. I hate thinking about it. It feels like if I think about it too much the universe will overhear and take it back, realizing it should never have happened; a cosmic screwup that I was idiotic enough to remember out loud, and now I'm caught. It feels like it's something I just need to accept and never mention again, just to be safe. So.

The end.

Just kidding.

(I'm going to tell you.)

I worked at a website before Peter—one of the ones people disliked until it was gone, at which point it had always been their favorite. I've worked at a few of this kind of website, typically right until their bitter end, but at this one I'd been laid off about ten months before it died, allowing me to be both sad and haughty at its many funerals. This job loss was once a source of great angst, but it made space in my life. It gave me time. It made me a freelance writer, which is a generous term for an unemployed person who is able to tend to a dog day and night.

At that point I lived alone in a Brooklyn neighborhood called Windsor Terrace. I still live there now, but with Peter. I moved to Windsor Terrace because I found rent there I could afford, but I've come to love its peacefully post-apocalyptic vibe. With blocks and blocks of one- and two-family homes, some even featuring driveways, the area is almost suburban in its loneliness, and in the fact that you have to leave it in order to do anything fun. On most afternoons you'd go on a walk in the neighborhood and see no one, save for maybe the large Great Dane who somehow always managed to escape his family's front gate to stroll around as if he were a simple Brooklyn podcaster. Gone to fetch ambient tone for your squirrel-and-bird podcast again, hm, Great Dane? Then you'd escort him back. Friends won't come to visit you because it's too far away, and when they do they say things like, "It's so . . . ah, peaceful here," by which they mean post-apocalyptic, and you say, "Thank you. Maybe *you* should move here." And they say, "Ahh, ha . . . uh, maybe!"

One of the loveliest parts of Windsor Terrace, along with the quiet so tranquil it makes you wonder *Oh no, has everyone died?*, is Sean Casey Animal Rescue. The rescue is about a block away from where I lived, and during the day they allow volunteers to stop by and sign out dogs to take for walks. While I was a dogless freelancer, I'd walk a dog every afternoon; picking up their poop, defending their right to pee (not everyone was as happy as I was to live in the proximity of an animal rescue), cooing and giving them affection. Much to the rescue staff's relief, I eventually stopped crying after handing them back post-walk.

Lovelier still, another rescue is headquartered about a block away, a rescue called Badass Brooklyn. I decided I wanted to be a foster there after seeing a photo of a basset hound on their website. It's a quite tantalizing idea, I'm sure you agree: a basset hound in my apartment. A basset hound waddling around, sitting his big basset hound butt on the floor. Me asking a basset hound, "Does this look gross or should I wear it?" Me picking up the basset hound and holding his whole body. A basset hound waiting for his forever home while I kiss his big droopy face.

The dog adoption process in New York City can be quite laborious, for good reason—I know a lot of good people who should absolutely not have a dog—and the foster application process is equally so. I filled out a long questionnaire detailing my lifestyle, my experience with dogs, and my expectations for my experience as a foster. I tried to make myself look good. For example, I'd recently convinced Tony Hawk to attempt to teach me how to ollie in under an hour for an article. I added this fact to the application. I guess I imagined them thinking, *Well, Tony Hawk wouldn't attempt to teach an* irresponsible *person how to ollie in under an hour.* (They never confirmed whether this helped.) (And, ultimately, Tony Hawk was only sort of able to teach me how to ollie.) (I blame that failure entirely on Tony Hawk.) I also had to include the phone numbers, email addresses, and job descriptions of three references. If those all checked out, I'd have an apartment visit, so someone from the rescue could make sure my living situation was tenable. This made me very nervous.

My apartment was a one-bedroom on the second floor of a house on a tree-lined street. It had three big windows that looked right out onto trees whose blooming process, after six years of living there, I'd become intimately acquainted with. They were the sort that dropped red shit everywhere. It was really wonderful, to see the tree growing its little red shit that it would drop everywhere, right before it began to grow its green leaves. Such a pleasure to behold...all that red shit everywhere in the spring.

Next to my bedroom I had a teeny-tiny living room, just big enough to fit a love seat and a TV, and then an oddly large kitchen. It made the apartment good for parties, as people tend to hang out in the kitchen anyway, and good for cooking, but otherwise I did tend to wish there weren't so much weird empty space in the gigantic kitchen compared with the teeny-tiny adjacent living room. I had a dinner table in there, if you can imagine. A dinner table in a one-bedroom apartment in Brooklyn. Kitchen largeness relative to the other rooms in one's apartment, I hoped, would be paramount in the foster approval decision.

A volunteer with the rescue came by to do the home visit. I pictured her snooping through my drawers, saying things like, *You don't separate your pajama shirts and non-pajama shirts? How do you expect to take care of a dog?* Looking at the old, framed portrait of a young man in a suit that I bought for $12 at a yard sale and asking, *Why haven't you burned this haunted object?* Seeing stacks of mail indicating that I don't seem to open the majority of my mail and commenting with suspicion, *You don't seem to open...the majority of your mail.*

She looked through the apartment gingerly and told me if I were assigned a puppy I would need a better system for keeping my recycling, as my system at that time was to put it on the ground, and a puppy would tear it apart. Otherwise everything checked out. We sat down to chat in the living room and she asked me, with some, ultimately prescient, suspicion, why I thought I wanted to be a foster. I explained that I wanted to care for a dog, but didn't feel like I could, at that point, commit to doing it forever. I didn't feel particularly settled, and I wasn't particularly happy with the life I'd built for myself; I assumed big changes had to be coming. A new job, big opportunities, a guy I wanted to marry. I didn't know if a dog would always fit. She told me she could never do it, "you know, get to know a dog and then send him off." I didn't think much of the warning.

Foster training was a one-day seminar at the Windsor

Terrace headquarters that involved learning how to teach dogs to walk on a leash, to go to their crate, and to be quiet. As a foster, part of your job was to train the dogs, ease them into city life, and make them more adoptable. "You're going to want to adopt the first dog assigned to you," the no-nonsense Badass Brooklyn employee in charge of the training told us. "But know that we have a strict no-foster-to-adopt rule." Got it. "Some of you will still ask," she said, "and we will tell you no."

Badass has this rule because the rescue doesn't have a brick-and-mortar location at which their dogs can live, and they rely on their fosters to enable them to rescue and temporarily home the dogs. It makes sense. Allowing these fosters to adopt would, more often than not, put their home out of commission. Plus, they have a stable of wannabe-adopters waiting to find their own special friend who would not be aided by a foster swooping in and adopting their dog out from under them. I'm telling you this to make sure you know that I am aware about why I was wrong to do what I did. That said I do need you to remember that you like me and you're on my side.

I was told the first dog I'd be looking after was named Jon Hamm. (The rescue gives all the dogs celebrity names. I ultimately never got a chance to meet this dog so I can't confirm any similarity to the human version, however I'm willing to bet he was equally suited for both comedy and drama.) I was perfectly fine with the idea of fostering Jon

Hamm, as well as the idea of calling out to him in public: JON HAMM!

That I would be taking care of Jon Hamm changed after a get-to-know-you portion of the day revealed that I worked from home. Ah-*huh*. In that case, I'd be taking care of Peter Parker, who needed to urinate an unreasonable number of times per day, which is none of your business, due to the heartworm medicine he was taking. His current foster couldn't handle all the peeing, and they were looking for the right person, free of the sort of responsibilities that force one to regularly leave her house for either work or socializing, to take over. A writer was the natural choice.

At home, I set up my space for him. I put his crate in my room, and put a few towels and a bedsheet inside to make it softer. I set up a plush doggy bed, and his food and water bowl. I scattered the dog toys I'd bought. I tapped my foot, I waited impatiently. His former foster, a woman named Megan, dropped him off at my apartment in the late afternoon the next day, and looked physically pained to do so. *Oh, Peter...good-bye*, she told him. *Lady, get over it*, I thought. In a plastic bag, she gave me a can of dog food, his medicine, and an alternate leash. Then she was on her way, and we were alone.

We were instructed to put the dogs in their prepared crates immediately upon receiving them, so they could calm down and adjust to their new location. I put him in and he lay down. We listened to the birds chirp outside and looked at each other. Sometimes he would look around the apartment, and sometimes he would put his head down, completely stoic, every move measured and in silence. I just stared at him.

A bit later I let him out, and he investigated his new surroundings. He sat in his bed, he chewed on his new bone. I fed him dinner and he ate it *very* fast. It felt strange to suddenly have a dog in my apartment. A gentle little soul, quietly alive with me. Sitting in my small living room. Looking at me with his big, sweet eyes. Padding around.

Fuck.

In the following days I tried to convince myself that I did not desperately need to adopt Peter, and that I was just going through the sort of new foster symptoms they warned about. Maybe I would feel this way about any dog; maybe we weren't unusually linked. It soon became clear, though, that I in fact did desperately need to adopt Peter. This realization occurred after a gynecologist appointment. I understand that is maybe too much information, but these happen to be the facts of the situation and I do hope it at least makes any prudes reading this uncomfortable. During the appointment the doctor asked if I had a history of cancer on either side of my family and I told her yes, both sides. She looked at me like I'd made a horrible mistake, as if I'd accidentally requested the cancer be on both sides after misreading some sort of form—a grievous error, indeed. Curse my carelessness!

The look lingered with me, and the simmering anxiety spilled over into panic when I got a message from her on my phone a few days after my appointment, explaining nothing and asking me to call her back. I don't understand why doctors do this. If any doctors are reading this—please do not do this. It's not only the lack of information, but the apparent belief that it is possible to just *call them back*. Instead of, *This is Dr. Whomever calling for Kelly. Give me a call back when you can*, how about:

This is Dr. Whomever, and [either everything is fine or everything is not fine]. You are [either fine or dying]. With the state of health care in our country, this is going to cost you [either a small but annoying amount, as it seems like the insurance you pay for should cover it, or all of your money and much of the money of your loved ones and potentially some money from kind strangers online]. [Sorry.] [You can attempt to call me back but good luck.]

It would at least be more honest. Anyway, I was sobbing, panicked, frantically trying to get in touch with her via the hospital's labyrinthine phone system. My sobbing got more violent as I was transferred to further and further areas of the hospital, and finally a receptionist I scared agreed to just forward me to the doctor's personal office telephone. Thank you. As I sat there hyperventilating, Peter, who was sitting next to me on the couch, pushed his body closer and closer to me, knowing something was wrong and doing his best to snuff out the flame of it. He stuck his sweet head under my arm, then right in my face, making direct eye contact, and eventually he forced his whole little cannonball body right on top of my lap. The doctor told me she had to call me back, and while I waited I held Peter and cried. He was pushing his body onto mine with force, making himself weightier, as if to communicate, *I'm here, I'm here, I'm here, I'm here.*

The phone call ended up being about some fucking insurance thing.

In what I believe is a remarkably self-controlled move—and I do think you're going to be impressed—I waited ten days after getting Peter before reaching out to the rescue to beg them to let me adopt him. He was on crate rest for the extent of it, so he couldn't do much in the way of dog-like activity, but we walked. I bought him toys and we played. We sat on the bed together, and he rested his head on my shoulder. I talked to him, and I told him that I know it might seem too soon to say it, and he didn't need to say it back, but I loved him. I looked at him and he looked at me. We existed and got to know each other. He was otherworldly.

"Hi, I'm fostering Peter," I emailed on the tenth day. It still exists in my Gmail, nauseatingly. "I know it was explained very clearly that fosters aren't able to adopt their foster dogs, and then explained again, and it was then explained that probably some will email to ask anyway and they will be turned down. That is the process I'm entering into right now."

Of course, I was turned down.

"I am not surprised by your desire to adopt Peter Parker as he is a charmer!" the rescue wrote. "But you are correct in assuming what our response will be. Peter Parker does have interest from adopters and in order to be fair to those who went through the long process of being approved to adopt we must allow them that chance before considering a foster for adoption."

The email was, I think, the second-to-worst part of my desperate quest for Peter. The worst part came the next day. The rescue held regular adoption events, during which fosters would drop off their dogs at a location for a few hours for potential adopters to meet them and, maybe, adopt them right on the spot. A blissfully wonderful and, in my case, nightmarishly horrifying concept. The only thing keeping me upright was the fact that Peter was still taking his heartworm medication, and I was told he was ineligible for adoption until he completed the prescribed course.

That bit of a safety net keeping my heart from sinking out of my body and into a grave disappeared as soon as I attempted to check Peter in. The orange-vested check-in volunteer asked callously (in my memory; I'm sure my emotional state was tainting it and actually she was just being normal): "You want to say goodbye in case he's adopted today?" What the fuck, no. What the fuck? No! I choked out the thing about... he's on heartworm medicine...and the rest of the pills are at home?...and they said...so I don't think he can get adopted today because...*they said!* She checked with another volunteer and begrudgingly (in my memory) confirmed I was right.

While I waited elsewhere for strangers to see if they wanted to adopt the dog I knew I loved, I got a sad sandwich and cried into it. It was pathetic. I made a friend get a drink with me, which was slightly less pathetic, because at least I wasn't alone, and at least I was drinking, but it *was* the early afternoon, and in any case all I could think about was Peter. Who was he meeting? What was he thinking? What was happening with my dog?

I tried to tell myself that if it were meant to be, it would happen. He would be mine. And if it weren't, then he wouldn't. He would be someone else's, and my dog would be another dog. There wasn't much else to console myself with, so I had to make do.

When I arrived at the scheduled pickup time it was raining, which was too on-the-nose. I found Peter sitting on the curb with a man. And it wasn't, like, a special man—maybe some kind of man who deserved him. It was just some normal man. He was tall and had jeans and brown hair. A volunteer told me this man was potentially interested in adopting Peter, and could I please answer any questions he might have?

We introduced ourselves, and he had one question. No, it was not, *How did Peter get to be so perfect, oh my god?* It was not, *How does this sweet dog even exist?* It was not, *Can you believe our luck, not only getting to reside on the planet at the same time as this gentle soul, but to have even gotten to spend time with him?* It was:

"Is he good to stay home by himself?"

Can you believe that?

I told him, yeah, he was great. He was quiet. He was good.

I hated that man. Truly, I hated him. I still do. He remains one of my greatest enemies even though I know nothing about him other than that he wanted to adopt a dog, which is actually nice.

As Peter and I left the grounds of the adoption event we were stopped by a woman who worked with the rescue. She knew Peter, and stopped me to ask how he was doing, startled to suddenly be in a situation in which she had to console a silently crying woman. She asked what was wrong and I said I wanted to adopt him, but couldn't. She made a face that expressed both sadness and the understandable desire for the interaction to be over, and we parted ways.

A few days later I got an email.

Hello Kelly—I wanted to touch base again about this. Have you submitted an application? If you have not I would suggest you get it on file in case.

The rescue wanted to cover all the bases in the event that the parties interested in adopting Peter backed out.

Though the foolishness these parties would have to display in such a decision was beyond my ability to conceive, I filled out the forms immediately. Waiting for their response was excruciating. Hopelessness is difficult but at least it's certain; hope without the power to change the outcome either way is torture. From what I can remember, I think that's what they kept singing about in *Les Misérables*.

It took about a week for them to get back to me.

> The foster team had let us know you were interested in adopting Peter. Because you have not been fostering with us for very long and we don't have a lot of experience with you in the foster program, we do need to go through a thorough review of your adoption application.

I was floored—absolutely ecstatic while trying to remain wholly unconvinced that he would ever be mine so as to not tempt fate with unearned assuredness, which is a trick I learned from growing up Catholic. Over the next few days my references were checked. I made sure to list my most prestigious friends: the Harvard graduate who worked at the *New Yorker*, the doctor who'd written a book; the guy who hosted a humor podcast that was actually fairly popular among those interested in the inner workings of comedy. Then I had another home visit. Two days later I heard back.

Hi Kelly,

We just received your home visit report and you are now approved to adopt—congratulations!!

After an initial excited response, I sent an immediate follow-up: Wait, I was approved to adopt *Peter*, right? Not just in general?

Yes! You are approved to adopt Peter:).

I've reached out to the rescue to ask what happened between the no I received and the request for an adoption application. They haven't told me. I assume they're likely too busy homing dogs to attempt to recount the particulars of an errant foster adoption from several years ago. But I do wonder about it. Did they take pity on me? Was it because of the woman I spoke to at the event? Was there a miscommunication between the foster team and the adoption team? Did it actually happen that Peter didn't have interest from other potential adopters? Did the man at the adoption event turn out to be a murderer, just as I immediately suspected he was?

At this point it seems like I'll never know. But I'm so grateful for it, settled comfortably with Peter in the life we've built for ourselves.

(Plus I bet it was the last one.)

Chapter 2

WHAT DOES MY DOG'S DNA SAY ABOUT HIM?

Everyone thinks Peter is a puppy. His large, wide-set eyes; small, soft body; and playful demeanor belie his maturity and emotional depth—attributes that become obvious once you get to know him. The truth is he was estimated to be about three when I adopted him, though the exact date of his birth, like that of many rescue dogs, is lost. He looks, to my eye, like some sort of a Labrador-terrier mix, with a soulful amber gaze, spunky little foldy ears, and an itty-bitty little nosey. I love him very much.

Until recently, though, his age and breed were up for debate. This was evidenced by an apparent dog expert at the local dog park one morning, when Peter was about four. "No," he said, shaking his head, after asking for the details of my dog. "My dog looked like that when she was a puppy, and now she looks like this." He gestured to his large pit-bull-looking sweetie who, though beautiful, looked nothing like my small Labrador-looking sweetie whom I love so much and for whom I would die. "Well ... he's about four," I told him, hiding my annoyance well as I am extremely calm. "No. I don't think so," he said.

Hm.

The main reason I wanted to DNA test my dog was to shove the results in this rude man's goddamn rude fuckin' face, wherever he is. Probably hell!

At-home dog DNA testing was made possible after the dog genome was sequenced in 2005 from the DNA of a female boxer named Tasha. Thank you, Tasha. This information provided a jumping-off point to map to the genomes of other dog breeds and their markers of genetic diseases, as well as some stuff about human diseases that frankly I do not think I should be the one to explain to you; you may seek that information out yourself.

"Of the more than fifty-five hundred mammals living today, dogs are arguably the most remarkable," said Eric Lander, senior author of the dog genome sequencing study and professor of biology at MIT. I agree. "The incredible physical and behavioral diversity of dogs—from Chihuahuas to Great Danes—is encoded in their genomes. It can uniquely help us understand embryonic development, neurobiology, human disease, and the basis of evolution." Wild stuff.

For my at-home dog DNA test I picked Embark, which, according to Embark, puts to use "over 20 times more genetic information than any other test on the market." They use more than two hundred thousand genetic markers to establish your dog's breed, or breed mix, and more than 175 genetic health and trait tests to establish whether your dog is at risk for or a carrier of genetic disease. I chose it because at $189 it was the most expensive option, and I was not paying for it. (I was writing about it for a website.) Of the many tests currently on the market, Embark's main competitor is Wisdom Panel 4.0, which only uses two thousand genetic markers and costs only $84.99. Yeah right. DNA My Dog, the next-most-popular according to various online lists, doesn't even give you a number of genetic markers it uses and costs a measly $68.98. Please.

Embark's kit comes with a swab. You hold the swab to the inside of your dog's cheek for a few seconds, which they dislike very much, and then you put it into the sample tube, and then you send it back. It's a simple process that I was positive I would screw up, but somehow did not. Peter fought with the swab, and didn't allow me to hold it in his mouth for the appropriate amount of time, but it still worked. They get the results to you in about two months, which is so long.

Before he was a foster with Badass Brooklyn, Peter was a stray in southeast Georgia. (I was also born in Georgia, when my family was stationed at the army base in Augusta.) The stray dog population is very large there, so Badass makes regular trips to bring back dogs to be adopted in New York. Peter was found and taken to a kill shelter in a town called Mount Vernon, one that could only hold about ten or twelve dogs at a time. The shelter tries to hold on to the dogs that have the best chance of being adopted. The rest are euthanized. An animal welfare group in nearby Toombs County called the Sweet Onion Animal Protection Society (SOAPS) regularly tries to remove as many dogs as they can before that happens, to be placed in foster homes and eventually adopted.

While awaiting the results of Peter's DNA test, I reached out to SOAPS director, Therisa Ingley, to see if the organization had any information about his pre-Brooklyn life. They had a little, from February 2017:

"When Badass was visiting last February, we visited the shelter and they fell in love with Peter Parker. He had been picked up as a stray and had been there for a while," she said. "Very few dogs from shelters get adopted here because there are just so many. Badass fell in love with his gentle nature and he was pulled to go back with them."

He lived for about three years before I knew him. It really kills me that I wasn't able to protect him during that time, and that I'll never really know what his life was like. However, I plan to teach him how to talk and I will update you once he tells me.

I'd like to take some time to describe Peter. When I talk about him I always think of the line from J. R. Ackerley's *My Dog Tulip*: "It is necessary to add that she is beautiful." The context isn't ever the same (Ackerley had just finished gently describing what most would likely deem bad behavior from his beloved dog, Tulip, and was about to note that she didn't like being petted), but the necessity is there. He is beautiful; it would be a sin of omission to withhold it. His black hair is very shiny—strangers are sometimes irritated that I won't tell them what they presume to be my secret about what I feed him to get his coat so lustrous, but I'm sorry, it is proprietary information. (The secret is that he's constructed entirely from eyelash wishes.)

He has velvet ears that move around like satellites, but in their at-rest position the left is folded and the right is perked. His amber eyes are stunningly bright, and are surrounded, like a human's, by an always-visible sclera. His nose—I can't even speak of it; its virtue is beyond description. He has a spotted tongue, which is one of my favorite of his features, though when I first took him in I frantically searched the internet about "DOG SPOTTED TONGUE WHY," worried it meant I'd done something to him that made him sick. I'd never seen one before. It looks like he ate a pen. It is beautiful.

When he walks down the stairs, at his moderately paced gentleman's trot, you can tell he's a bit bowlegged. He has the heart of an angel and the soul of a poet, and there's a hint of sadness to him that makes you want to protect him against all the world's harshness. He has whiskers that are so prominent they make you second-guess whether whiskers are a typical dog trait, or whether he could potentially be part mouse. He will sit his big, fat butt on your lap like he's tiny, when he actually weighs twenty-seven pounds. He's affectionate, but not needy. "He's just so…kind," is how a cousin of mine once described him, and it's true: He's just so kind. Also he loves to burrow under the covers, and he loves to sleep with his head on a pillow like a tiny little man.

I wanted to know what he is because I want to know everything I can about him. I want to know why he's a little bowlegged. I want to know why he has a spotted tongue. I want to know why he's so sweet, I want to know why he's so gentle. I didn't imagine the DNA test would unveil all of his secrets, but I love him and I wanted to know whatever the DNA test could tell me. Plus, I wanted to shove the information in the face of any goddamn rude know-it-alls I came across in the future.

But were there any practical reasons to get his DNA tested? I reached out to Dr. Ann Hohenhaus, staff doctor at New York City's Animal Medical Center, to ask.

"Well, I think that it depends," she said. "You can use DNA testing for a lot of things. One thing is for fun." Meaning, to find out what kind of a little man Peter is and then shove it in the face of somebody who thinks they know better. "The second is that we've been using DNA tests in dogs for a long time to diagnose specific diseases…With a particular breed and a particular set of clinical signs, a DNA test may be a very efficient way to make a diagnosis in a patient."

While I was impatiently awaiting the results of my DNA test, this was something that was haunting me. What if the DNA test told me Peter was sick? He didn't seem sick. But what if maybe he was going to be sick in the future? I also worried about how I would write around it here. Maybe I would attempt to feature it as a poignant look at the impermanence of life, but, in contrast, the permanence of love—how his love will always be with me, and mine with him, no matter what. That would have been quite touching. Luckily I do not have to travel down this heart-wrenching road, because after six agonizing weeks of waiting, I received Peter's impressive results.

Peter tested clear for the 165 genetic conditions for which Embark scans, including 28 that are common in his breed mix, like congenital hypothyroidism, progressive retinal atrophy, and muscular dystrophy. Huh. *Not even at risk for any of them?* I wondered. *Did I do it wrong?* I wondered. "Did I do it wrong?" I asked Dr. Hohenhaus.

"I'm not surprised your dog was negative for those diseases, because those genetic diseases don't occur very often in mixed-breed dogs," she said. Oh. "That's not to say they never do—I've diagnosed genetic disease in a mixed-breed dog. The disease normally occurred in the springer spaniel and this dog was a black-and-white short-haired thing, and it had the same genetic mutation. But that's the only time I've ever done that. So, it occurs but it's rare."

Still, she said there can be danger in taking negative results of the at-home swab test as gospel. The tests typically look for a single mutation, and if your dog's disease (say pyruvate kinase deficiency, which affects red blood cells and has several mutations across different breeds) has a mutation that hasn't been discovered yet—even if he presents symptoms that would be obvious to a veterinarian—it won't catch it. Plus, a cheek swab test means a bacteria-laden sample: "When I do DNA testing, I take a blood sample and send it in. And a blood sample is inherently 'cleaner,' in quotes, than if you do a home DNA test with a cheek swab," Hohenhaus told me. "So that test has some inherent issues, because you have the DNA of the bacteria in the dog's mouth along with the dog's DNA, in that sample. And so I think that there is probably an opportunity for a sample that's harder to read if there's a lot of bacteria in the mouth. I think really the at-home DNA testing is not as much for disease as it is for the fun."

That seems right. Mostly what you're looking for when you're giving your dog a DNA test you ordered from the internet, I believe, is the fun of finding out the fun little mystery of who he is, and then the fun of telling all of your friends about it at every opportunity, even though they do not care at all that your dog is 3 percent poodle. *Can you believe it? Three percent poodle! I mean, I don't see it at all, do you? Do you want to see another picture? Let me show you this one I took the other day. I think you can kind of see some poodle there. Maybe around the snout? You know—well, I was looking into poodles, and, in fact—*

Anyway, speaking of the fun little mystery of who he is, do you want to know what Peter is? Oh my god. Oh my god. Oh my god. Are you ready? Do you have your guess? Maybe you should take some time to go over what I've told you about Peter to make sure your guess is the guess you want to go with. Hm? Let's see:

√ Soul of a poet
√ Kind
√ Always-visible sclera
√ Man at the park thought he knew more about him
    than I did
√ Nose beyond description

Okay, do you have your guess? Here it is, according to the test:

19.7% Labrador Retriever
15.4% Chihuahua
12.9% Golden Retriever
12.8% Dachshund
12.2% Rat Terrier
9.6% Miniature Schnauzer
7.1% American Staffordshire Terrier
10.3% Supermutt

He is, as you can see, so many things. A buffet of breeds. A smörgåsbord of strains. A platter of Peter, though that one sounds somewhat violent and I'd like to retract it, thank you. There he is. My little Peterman, a true original. (If you're wondering what "supermutt" means, according to Embark it means that there may be "small amounts of DNA from these distant ancestors": chowchow, dalmatian, and miniature pinscher. My little supermutt.)

He's all there. The basic body structure of a Labrador retriever. The smaller stature of a Chihuahua. The intelligent, calm demeanor of a golden retriever. The love of burrowing of the small-prey-hunter dachshund. The wide-set eyes and expressive ears of a rat terrier. The sociability of the miniature schnauzer. The wide chest and slightly bowed back legs of the American Staffordshire terrier. The spotted tongue of the chowchow.

I asked Dr. Hohenhaus if there's anything practical to be gleaned from the breeds that go into a mutt, and she said the area of study was still in flux. She wasn't sure the evidence was out there—yet. In the future, she said, "We'll know better how to use that information." Maybe we'll be able to use it to fine-tune their diet, or to have more insight into their health problems, or to figure out whether they would prefer a hard bitey toy or a soft squeaky toy. I don't know. Perhaps you are living in the future as you read this, and you *do* know, and you're thinking, *She was not right*. Well. If so, I congratulate you on your ability to remain alive while, I imagine, the planet deteriorates around you. But for now, I at least know how I'll use this information, which is: against rude men who think they know more about my dog than I do at the dog park.

CHAPTER 2.5: IS IT FUCKED UP TO THROW AWAY A WHISKER?

It's very alarming to find a disembodied whisker. A vibrissa. Thick and coarse with a bulbous root, sensitive and packed with nerves, not to evoke a penis. Formerly used to aid in a dog's navigation, now discarded to be found by a human and...what? Buried in a grave? Cremated? Kept in a special locked box labeled JUST SOMETHING NORMAL in case anyone finds it?

Dogs lose whiskers naturally, if not particularly often, but the resulting cleanup feels different from cleaning up, say, dog hair. At least to me. They play a vital part in how dogs interact with the world, and they're just so...thick. I know I already said they were thick, but I feel like I need to repeat it. It's odd to find them on the ground, or in your bed, or wherever, and it seems fucked up to just throw them away; like you're throwing away a finger. Or a baby tooth. I know it's also odd to come across a box of disembodied baby teeth, but thinking about it now, it would seem even odder to throw one away. So what do you do?

Typically whenever I find one of Peter's whiskers I just sort of set it aside. Not for keeping, really, just to put off actively throwing it away. Eventually the whisker gets knocked to the floor, and I do sweep it up and dispose of it unknowingly, but at least I don't have to make the decision to do it in the moment. The poor felled whisker. Oh, I miss him!

Curious about whether I'm psycho or normal, I reached out to Laure Hoenen, a French bioethicist specialized in animal ethics (I'm telling you she's French so you can imagine her answers in the correct accent). She spoke to me over a free video chatting system that I'd never heard of before and did not trust the efficacy of, but that worked reasonably well, and which I apologize for doubting. Hoenen has a cat, and she agreed that she has a different reaction to picking up her cat's discarded whiskers than she does her cat's discarded hair. She said, regarding her reaction upon finding a whisker: "... I do stop."

She continued, "I don't find it odd, I just find it fascinating. And I get your questioning. Maybe it's because there are so few of them—and because we don't have them. And they're very strong. I don't know how dog ones are, but the cat ones are very . . . strong? Rigid. It's a strong material." I know!

She asked if I felt the same way about nails, pointing out a difference between dogs and cats that, to be honest, I did not know about until she told me. Cats periodically shed the outer layer of their claws, like snakes do with their skin; dogs do not. I'm not sure how I hadn't come across this fact about cats just as a person in the world, but at least I know it now, and isn't it nice to learn something new. I don't care much about throwing out my dog's nail clippings, but Hoenen said she has the same reaction to finding these nail layers as she does to finding stray whiskers. "If I'm cleaning my house and I find one on the floor . . . it stops my movement for a second. With hair it's just like, oh, I need to clean the house, there are hairs everywhere. But it's not the same thought process."

In animal ethics, she told me, decision-making typically goes like this: They think about how we deal with situations in animals, how we deal with the same situation in humans, whether there is a difference, and what the difference is based on. "So I'm like—okay, we don't have whiskers. That's the first point. But we have other body parts that are similar, like fingernails. They're not the same, but they're useful, to scratch, to open things, et cetera. And the way we dispose of them would be trash." She pointed out that the same is true if you get something like your appendix removed at the hospital, though with human stuff there's the matter of privacy to consider. "Like your DNA. If anybody gets your DNA, especially today, they can have access to information about you. But those questions don't really matter for animals. I'm not sure they have a sense of DNA privacy.

"Another way you can look at this is thinking about who the stakeholders are. Who are the parties involved, and what are their interests? Once you know that, you can kind of balance them to make your decision." In this case she said the stakeholders would be me and Peter. "And once the whiskers fall out, I don't think the dog cares that much. So that's their interest." She said "my" interest, as in the human's, would depend on the human. She, for example, doesn't think about these things too much. She stops to consider the whisker, and moves on. "You think," she said, about me, "...um, more about it." Mmhm. "So I think it depends on the human person, as well. We have to look at how the humans feel about it."

Because there haven't been studies into the ethics surrounding dog whiskers, she said it might be interesting to see how Peter reacts to one of his own once it's fallen out, as a behavioral study. "You can see how he reacts to the whiskers, when you find one. That would be interesting. If he just sees one in his path, maybe that would be different. If you present it, maybe he would be interested."

The next time I found an abandoned whisker, I put it in front of Peter's face. He seemed momentarily curious, and made a small sniff at the air in front of it. Then he lost interest. After I placed the whisker on the ground, he didn't notice it at all.

"From an ethical standing I don't see anything wrong with just trashing the whiskers," Hoenen said. "But that doesn't mean the question is irrelevant."

SO THERE!

Chapter 3

IS MY DOG A FESTIVAL-TYPE?

Entrants to Toronto, Ontario's sixteenth annual Woofstock dog festival were greeted with a threat:

DON'T DISAPPOINT YOUR DOG!

AHH! The message appeared on a large sign and it was odd both because the text was pink, a choice clearly intended to make it seem like the sign wasn't already angry with us, and because it was positioned to yell exclusively at those who had already paid $16 to enter a festival called Woofstock. These are the people already won over by the threat of disappointing their dog, I can assure you. These people have that fear in their bones. These are the people who hear the warning *DON'T DISAPPOINT YOUR DOG!* ringing in their ears as they lie awake in the section of their bed not taken up by their dog; they feel it when he doesn't seem to be enjoying the treat they baked for him, or when the eyes on the dog portrait they commissioned don't convey a sufficient amount of empathy—*DON'T DISAPPOINT YOUR DOG!* Oh my god! I'm sorry! I SWEAR TO GOD I'M TRYING SO HARD NOT TO!

Woofstock is, according to Woofstock, "the largest festival for dogs in North America." I can't find any evidence to discount this claim, and I have no reason to doubt Woofstock or its promoters, so I choose to believe it. You may doubt it if that is your nature. To test them, I emailed a Woofstock representative to ask if they, by any chance, knew what the second-largest festival for dogs was in North America. It seems to me like they should keep track of these stats in order to maintain their standing, or to kindly relinquish it to another, larger dog festival. They replied: "Sorry, no."

I realize this does little to ease your doubt.

Still, the use of the superlative indicates that there are other, if not quite as large, festivals for dogs in North America, and this is true. There are many. There's Muttzanita in Manzanita, Oregon; DogFest San Diego in San Diego, California; BARKtoberfest in Gilbert, Arizona. There's also an annual Woofstock festival in Voorhees, New Jersey, which we will never speak of again out of respect for our Woofstock, which is to say the Woofstock that Peter and I have already attended. There's also a festival called DoggieStock Music Festival in North Bend, Washington, which I commend for its alternative, if incorrect, take on the Woodstock pun.

All the festivals are sort of the same. They usually include some sort of dog parade, an invitation to dress your dog up in an undignified costume, vendors selling treats or otherwise dog-related items of varying uselessness, and maybe some dog sports and a doggy talent show. They're usually held to raise money for animal rescues or dog-related charities, and are advertised to be "as much for the human as for the dog," the charity aspect serving to help quiet the part of your mind that might be tempted to think they're a bit more for the former.

You might be wondering why, if dog festivals are held all over, Peter and I chose to go to one that was so far away that it is insane, and also in a different country. Well. Like I said, it is theoretically the largest one in North America, which sounds pretty impressive, you have to admit. Plus, at about nine hours away it was technically within driving distance. And aside from its largeness and reachability, Toronto's Woofstock is the dog festival that comes up most readily on search engines, and after I came across the fact of its existence, not going to it didn't particularly seem like an option. It was a challenge against which I refused to crumble. *Damn*, you can imagine me saying to Peter though in reality this scene did not take place. *Well. Obviously we have to go to this.*

Did you know that in car accidents unrestrained dogs can, upon impact, become a projectile that has the ability to decapitate the driver? It's true—my mom knows someone who died this exact way, she told me, after I expressed the anxiety I had about taking Peter on a long car trip. The possibility of decapitation did little to ease my worry.

I'm ashamed to admit that, until this outing, I hadn't been restraining Peter in the car. We take trips together semi-regularly—to cabins upstate, to rentals near the beach. But the fact that he is typically a very good little man had, in these scenarios, clouded my usual anxiety-fueled judgment, which one might rightfully assume would have lead me to put him in some sort of crash-proof doggy bubble. When we drove together, pre-Woofstock, he'd just sit in the backseat, looking out the window like a tiny passenger on a train trip toward a new life, enjoying the passing landscape. Or he would sleep. He didn't roam the car, he didn't jump into the front seat to distract me. He was just good, which, actually— was bad.

I don't want to bum you out with any of the terrifying specifics I consumed en masse in advance of this long car ride, but suffice to say it is not good to keep your dog unrestrained in your car. It's really not good to keep your dog unrestrained in a truck bed, and I would highly suggest not letting your dog stick his little head out of the car window. And, oh my god, definitely don't let your dog sit on your lap while driving, which—I'll have you know—17 percent of dog-owning drivers admitted to doing in a 2011 survey I came across from AAA. The National Highway Traffic Safety Administration does not keep track of pet-related car accidents, but the prevailing theory is that, if they did, the yearly number would be not insignificant. And this wouldn't even encompass the accidents in which free-roaming pets were merely victims. Be nervous, and adjust your behavior accordingly.

To assuage some of my worry, I purchased a sturdy new dog vest and a doggy seat belt that attached to that vest and anchored to the backseat headrest, plus I got a net for between the back and front seats that will definitely do nothing in an accident but still provides the level of mental comfort that spending money on something unnecessary can provide. I also took my car to the mechanic. I also purchased pet insurance. I also was unable to sleep through the night for over a month ahead of the trip, please leave me alone.

Peter, for his part, was not nervous. He loves the car wildly and freely, completely unaffected by the possibility that he might become a projectile able to sever a head. He can sense an impending car trip by various signifiers: packed bags, car keys jingling, outside clothes rather than pajamas, a general sense of panic. And when he does he gets immediate wiggle butt—butt wiggling all over the apartment, wiggle wiggle wiggle. Oh gosh, he is so excited. Oh gosh, we are going somewhere. Life has never felt as jubilant as this exact moment— we have never felt more alive, we have never *been* more alive. Though he did not know exactly that our trip was going to take us to my parents' house in Scranton, Pennsylvania, en route to a hotel in Buffalo, New York, en route to Woofstock in Toronto, Ontario, he knew we were headed somewhere—and that was enough!

Though I hate to ruin the suspense, I want to let you know we did not get into a fatal car accident going either to or from Woofstock. You may relax; I am not a ghost typing to you. We also didn't attach a BABY ON BOARD sticker to our car, though I was considering it. But I'm not sure if people really respect those stickers, and I definitely don't want to be the subject of errant disrespect on the road. Something we *did* do, though, is tell a lie to a man and as a result not have to pay the dog fee at the Hyatt Regency Buffalo, and I am so sorry, but before you judge us please let me explain.

When I checked in to the Hyatt Regency Buffalo the man at the desk asked if Peter was a service dog. Now, this is a hotel I booked specifically because it allowed dogs—or so I thought. (It did.) But places always lie about whether they allow dogs, and they particularly always lie on their stupid websites. "Thank you for coming but no, the restaurant no longer allow dogs on the deck outside; now you have to sit in the car with your dog and figure something else out on your phone while you're mad and starving and, likely, in an unfamiliar city." "Thank you for submitting your application and all relevant documents, but no, the apartment that said it allowed 'dogs and cats' actually only allows cats, or maybe you just don't make enough money, you'll never know, but you did hear dogs barking when you visited, and I think anyone would agree that that seems suspicious." "Thank you for asking but no, a couples massage cannot be for a dog and human even though they are technically a 'couple' of beings, and although our website did not specify this was a human-only activity it should have been assumed." Okay, fine.

So—the lie. (It's important to me to unburden myself and I thank you in advance for listening and understanding even if it is potentially not that interesting to you.) When the man asked if Peter was a service dog I said, "Umm...uh, yes."

The honest answer was no. However if I answered no and the response was "then he can't stay here," well, I think you can agree that I would have wished I'd lied. The nice man then waived the dog fee, which they do not apply to service dogs, and we slunk to our room in shame, watched *Pretty Woman* on cable, and had an admittedly very pleasant time. (Neither of us had ever seen it.) And I know what you're thinking—if you watch *Pretty Woman* on cable you don't get to see the sex parts. But we also rented it once we got home, and I think you're remembering the sex parts as hotter, more revealing, and more essential to the plot than they actually are.

I'm sorry, Hyatt Regency Buffalo. Please contact me or, better yet, my publisher if you really need that dog fee. I'm sure they would be happy to pay. I do think, though, that maybe you have enough money; you should potentially consider whether or not you're being greedy, and whether or not you should maybe drop the dog fee altogether. It's even possible that, newly ashamed, the Hyatt Regency Buffalo would like to refund our one-night stay entirely. In that case it was $114.10, and you may make the check out to me directly.

It was absolutely pouring the first morning of Woofstock. I'm not the sort of person who gets nervous driving in rain (yes I am), but this was the sort of rain that blinds you so the only things you can make out on the road—in this case Queen Elizabeth Way, along Lake Ontario—are the various horrifying car accidents. *That could be me*, you think, fully aware of how rude it is to think about yourself while looking at someone else's car accident. *That could be me, that could be me.* The one bright spot was explaining to the border patrol the reason for my visit. "*Woof*...stock?" Indeed, yes. Here on business, of course.

Toronto is a dog-loving city, which is to say it's a bit more dog-loving than a normal city, sort of in the way that Philadelphia or Seattle is, if that has any resonance with you. There are 250,000 licensed dogs within its limits, and from what I can tell—based on, admittedly, the two stores Peter and I visited—they are greeted warmly in most storefronts with cooing and treats. Based on the same bit of evidence-gathering I can say humans accompanying dogs are greeted less warmly, particularly after they explain that they've traveled all the way from Brooklyn, New York, for the local dog festival. "You came all the way here...for...that?" I was asked not once but every time I explained where I'd come all the way there for. And yes, indeed, I had come all the way there for that.

Woofstock takes place in a large open field in Woodbine Park, which is situated next to Woodbine Beach, which is situated on Lake Ontario. If you're wondering whether these locations were referred to as "Woofbine Park" and "Woofbine Beach" in any of the Woofstock promotional material, that's a good question, and they were not. Clearly a missed opportunity on Woofstock's part. (Lake Ontario could have been something like "Lake OntariooOOOOOo," to suggest a dog howling.)

After walking through the Woofstock gates, entrants came into view of the DON'T DISAPPOINT YOUR DOG! sign while being handed the festival's event guide. The event guide featured a charming, if familiar, slogan: DON'T DISAPPOINT YOUR DOG! This time it was placed rather effectively next to the image of a quite obviously disappointed bullmastiff. A very sad face on this sweet guy. Oh, buddy. I'm so sorry you're feeling disappointed. Maybe next year your caretaker will take you to Woofstock, which I suppose we are to assume is what you desire, rather than merely place your sad face on the cover of its hourly schedule.

Yes, dog-related guilt loomed large over Woofstock, as it does over most dog-related capitalist endeavors. It is so hard. You spend your life with this friend whom you love, and whom you are desperate to make happy. But what can you do? Guess at what flavor treat he likes. Decide on a winter coat for her without knowing very much about her taste, and while knowing very much that she hates to wear a winter coat. Like a clueless but well-meaning boyfriend typing "GOOD BIRTHDAY PRESENT GIRLFRIEND" into Google, you are left to take stabs in the dark at pleasing someone you love, but whom you will never fully know or understand. In this way, something like Woofstock can seem like a blessing. A list of ten great birthday presents any girlfriend will love for under $50. A whole festival created with the sole intent of pleasing your dog, by people whom you believe should know something about it, otherwise why would they put together the festival in the first place.

There was not a line to get into Woofstock on its first day, I have to admit. It had been raining, like I said, which made the dirt grounds of Woofstock 100 percent grass-mud, sometimes ineffectively covered in cardboard or hay. At one point I heard a man tell his young son (I assume it was his son) (could have been a seven-year-old acquaintance) that he hadn't come across any "landmines" yet, which I did not understand, until I did, and then I agreed. I hadn't, either, come across any "landmines" yet. This could either point to an inherent flaw in the idea of a dog festival, which is that dogs do not feel comfortable enough within its limits to shit, which makes me sad, or could be due to the overall, you know, mud-ness of the ground. If you step on a landmine but the results of the explosion mimic the horrific nature of the setting surrounding it, did you really step on a landmine at all? Something to consider.

Upon our arrival, at around noon, Peter and I mud-walked over to the in-progress event on the main stage, which was a dog fashion show. The stage was large and impressive, adorned with a…I've been trying to figure out how to describe it. Like a large 3-D logo…big cutout letters thing. You know what I mean? One of those things, like the sort of thing you see outside of a Comcast office building, and it says COMCAST. It said: WOOFSTOCK and then underneath, NORTH AMERICA'S LARGEST FESTIVAL FOR DOGS. It was quite impressive. The stage was flanked on both sides by signage displaying the logos of Woofstock's brand partners, which was also quite impressive, due both to the professional look of the signage and the number of brand partners they'd gathered, which was several. It was exactly what one would expect from North America's largest festival for dogs. This is what I'd come all the way here for. And isn't that normal!

Unlike the various Woofstock signage, the dog fashion show was amateur hour. Peter was immediately unimpressed. His little paws were in mud, while the dog models could barely even be coaxed to walk across the stage. And the clothes? Hideous. Garish. Ruffles, sparkles. The raincoats could be considered practical, sure, but certainly not dignified. Peter wouldn't even look at the stage, and I don't blame him. "What do you think, Pete?" I asked him. (I will frequently use the informal "Pete" in conversation.) He tugged on his action vest (he normally wears a blue collar, but in moments of action he prefers his vest) to go elsewhere, and I heard him loud and clear.

There were about two hundred vendors spread throughout the park, which sounds like a lot, but I'll have you know that number does include ten water zones. They had names like Designer Doggie, ÜberDog, Ultimutts, K9 Kulture, and Smoochy Poochy, and they offered just about anything you could ever "want" (by which, in general, I mean not particularly want) to buy for your dog: food, training, massages, sparkly dresses, pet sitting, energy healing, treats, little leather name tags that they'd stamp your dog's name into right in front of you (I bought this), and doggy ice cream (admittedly I also bought this). There were also several human food stands and a bunch of tents dedicated to rescue organizations. The vendors that made me feel the least guilty about the human-leaning concept of a dog festival were the ones that offered free treats in addition to their for-sale wares, and the best of those were the ones—treat companies, usually—that offered them in heaping buckets, although Peter disagreed.

When he's feeling uncertain, Peter does not like to eat treats. Sadly, he tends to feel uncertain whenever a stranger gives him a treat. I think this is very sweet, and that it shows an incredible survival instinct, and I'm proud of him for it, but it makes for some awkward encounters, as he is very cute, and, you see, people with treats are generally excited to give him one. He isn't rude to them. He allows them the pleasure of placing a treat in his mouth, accepts it gingerly, and delicately places it on the ground in front of him. Very polite. Thank you, but no thank you; I do not know you and furthermore I prefer to take all treats in my treat spot at home, which is the couch.

So he wouldn't eat any of the treats, even if I attempted to feed them to him myself. He was nervous. I understand. All around him dogs happily gobbled with abandon anything put in front of them, all different types of treats sure to give them a bit of diarrhea later, but Peter, like Bartleby before him, preferred not to. This even included a lime and blueberry doggy Popsicle that I swear to God looked so delicious the only thing keeping me from eating it myself was the fact that everyone around us also knew it was for dogs. Peter refused even a lick. You have to admire his restraint.

Luckily for us, there was a "Licensed Lounge." It was so fucking hot and muggy, and all Peter wanted was to be able to sit at a table with an umbrella and watch me enjoy a free lemonade and Tito's Vodka while waiting for the Mr. and Ms. Canine Canada Pageant to begin. Thankfully, Woofstock anticipated his desire. We waited there for a bit and caught our breath together; Peter under the table, me sitting in a chair. Here he was finally able to enjoy a nibble of the free treats I'd been hoarding in my backpack, stashing them away for when he felt more comfortable. It was quiet. Lying in the grass under a table, away from the crowd, was clearly the most at ease he'd felt all day.

At the table beside me, a tan, older, dogless man sat drinking his own free cocktail, taking in the scene. He had a mustache and the relaxed ease of Sam Elliott, cast in the role of a mustachioed Sam Elliott–type with a relaxed ease. He asked about Peter's age and breed (ageless, poet) and told me that his own dog, a larger breed I'd neglected to take note of, was back at home. Every year he comes to the first day of Woofstock alone, to stake out what activities his dog would like best and put together a game plan; the next day he takes his dog. "It's too hectic otherwise," he said. He had a point.

Scores for the Mr. and Ms. Canine Canada pageant (held on the main stage) would not be shared with participants because they were going to be tabulated based exclusively on looks, and the Woofstock judges did not want to hurt anyone's feelings. The host warned about this several times in the lead-up to the event. The pageant was based *exclusively* on looks—it was "purely physical," he said. Entrants would *not* receive their scores. Everyone is there to have a good time and knowing these scores might put a damper on that, as they are based *solely on looks*. I know what you're thinking: With his radiant eyes, perfectly folded ears, and body type reminiscent of a tiny horse, Peter is no doubt going to receive exactly the sort of brutally high score that necessitated the enforcement of this totalitarian restriction on information in the first place. And I agree.

Of course, we entered the competition.

In line to take the stage (when competing, human competitors walked their dogs in front of the judges' table on stage right and then across the length of the stage; quite humiliating, yes) we met an impassioned woman who immediately considered us her confidante, I suspect because we were standing the closest to her. She had a bit of a kerfuffle with another woman whose Pom, named Macchiato, kept approaching her blue-eyed Siberian husky, Akira. Akira did not like this, and my new friend was exasperated. "He's an asshole," she said of her dog, to Macchiato's owner. "He's fine off his leash but he's an asshole on his leash, that's why I'm trying to keep him close to me." She paused for a breath. "He doesn't like puppies especially, that's why I'm keeping him close to me." She then turned to me and gave a *what's wrong with this lady?* face, and I did the sort of shrug you do to say, *yeah, totally*, but between you and me I just wanted to stay out of it. Luckily fate intervened. While I attempted to figure out the polite social mechanics of the situation, Peter wandered over to Akira, which caused Akira to wander toward Peter. Oh no—this wasn't good. While I coaxed Peter back to me, Akira became upset. Immediately his owner turned on me; not even our proximity in line could save our friendship now. "I'm trying to keep him close to me," she said, as if sharing it for the first time. "He's fine off his leash," oh no, "but he's an asshole on his leash," oh no, "that's why I'm trying to keep him," oh no, "close to me," I KNOW!

A note about the attractiveness of the other dogs: They were all quite attractive. Conventionally. The sort of dogs whose owners make money or at least earn swag through social media.

The sort of dogs who are likely groomed somewhere other than an apartment bathtub. The sort of dogs who seem like they're bragging and should maybe just relax. I'm sure these dogs are just as wonderful as any non-model-esque dog, but participating in a beauty contest makes you question certain things. Like, why do these dogs get so much attention, huh? Why are the judges cooing all over them? Are they even charming? Do they even have a notably gentle disposition that becomes abundantly clear after spending some time with them? And for the love of god—*what kind of scores are they getting???*

The contest resulted in a four-way tie for Mr. Canine Canada. Peter—who is, as a reminder, one of his generation's great beauties—was not even among the four. After another round of voting it was whittled down to one: Akira.

That asshole.

I couldn't put Peter through any more Woofstock after his devastating loss, so we left to return the next day. When we woke on the morning of day two, the rains had migrated and the sun was shining, which made for a much more tightly packed Woofstock experience, similar, I imagine, to the sort of crowd Pupi Hendrix, Janis Joplick, and Bone Baez drew all those years ago, my apologies. Still, because we were there quite early, we were one of the first in line for the second day's most exciting new attraction: the lure course.

Are you familiar with lure courses? In them, a dog chases a piece of fabric or plastic (the lure), meant to remind them of a rabbit they'd like to murder. It's fastened to a line that is wrapped around several pulleys placed throughout an obstacle course. The lure can be tricky, cutting sharp corners and traveling through tires, et cetera, and dogs have a lot of fun chasing it. Each dog ahead of us was so tempted by the lyingly non-rabbit lure that they had to be physically restrained until they were officially allowed to run. It was very sweet. Once allowed, they zoomed around the course with glee, jumping, diving, turning, sprinting. We all had fun watching them (the line grew very long behind me while we waited for our turn) and I couldn't wait for Peter's moment to shine.

When it was finally our turn, Peter took his place in front of the lure. My heart was pounding. We waited for the lure to finally fly from its resting place, and then, finally—WHOOSH!—it was released! Peter took one look at it, turned around, sat on his little butt, and looked at me. *Hm? Yes?* His eyes seemed to ask: *Is this what you want me to do, sit here on my little butt? Or . . . am I supposed to be waiting for you to do something? If so, take your time.* The lure course operator suggested that he might be more into it if I ran with him at the beginning, so we tried. The lure flew ahead of us and I chased it, over a jump, down the course, around a corner, with Peter right beside me—oh gosh, I was really flying. When I thought he had enough emotional momentum, I stopped. Instantly, Peter also stopped. Oh, buddy. He did not want to do this, and once again I couldn't blame him. There was a lot of pressure. A big crowd. A piece of fabric that hardly looked anything like a rabbit, who are we kidding. His charm shone through his failure, still, and we left the course to a large round of applause from the crowd. We deserved it.

Just as Peter finished his brave display of lure course non-compliance, the band Three Dog Day (ha-ha) took the main stage. Because their performance was advertised as a concert for dogs, I expected the sort of loopy, trippy, relax-my-dog-style music available on YouTube and various music streaming services that you play when you leave the house, in case dogs actually do like it, in order to assuage some guilt. Instead they played regular for-human songs that had the word "dog" in them, beginning their set with "How Much Is That Doggy in the Window." A song that weighs the cost of a dog against his apparent worth is an odd choice to play to a crowd of dogs, in my opinion, but of course I would never attempt to police someone's art.

Up next on the DON'T DISAPPOINT YOUR DOG! schedule was the Fur-Tastic K9s Performance & Stunt Dog Team. While the dogs on the stunt team were certainly fur-tastic—leaping, catching Frisbees, uh...leaping—the most spirited moment came when a French bulldog beside me jumped, and jumped, and jumped, tricking his owner into lifting him up to "see" the performance. (The performance took place inside a four-foot-high gate, so Peter and most of the other dogs were not able to view it.) The French bulldog, playing his owner like a fool, then completed his plan by jumping from his owner's arms directly into the arena. Freedom! Freedom! FREEDOM TO JOIN THE FUR-TASTIC K9S PERFORMANCE & STUNT DOG TEAM!

(He was promptly removed.)

The dog talent show took place on the main stage. I guess I'm not sure the level of talent one should expect from a crowd of dogs gathered for the sake of enjoying a festival, but a few people had acts; ringers, there to scoop up all the glory for themselves. They had their dogs dance, jump on their backs, things like this. Most, however, did not have very well-defined talents, and I think that is just fine. One woman's dog, a very tiny Chihuahua, "punched" her in the face. Okay. The woman I respected the most got up onstage and announced her dog did not have a talent, and that they would be winging it. The dog did absolutely nothing, her promise was fulfilled, and I do believe she should have won. Peter did not compete because I think it should be obvious by now that he has too much self-respect.

It was hard to tell whether any of the dogs in attendance at Woofstock were getting much enjoyment out of it. Dogs can be very hard to read if you don't know them personally. They trotted around, they pulled on their leashes toward each other, they gobbled down treats. The humans looked on a gradient from delighted to aggrieved: The festival was crowded, it was hot, the dirt was still mud. But there were a lot of dogs around, and it was certainly the largest group of people I've ever encountered that knew the appropriate way to greet a new dog was to let him first sniff the back of your hand.

In between Woofstock's activities I wandered around the booths in an attempt to find the "celebrity dog" tent. It was surprisingly difficult to find, but not for an interesting reason, only because I'm bad at reading any sort of map. Sorry, maybe I shouldn't have been so forthcoming about that. Regardless, I'd like to share with you a Woofstock-supplied bio for one of the dogs I missed due to my incompetence. His name is Ryder the Samoyed:

> Ryder the Samoyed is the h*ckin floofiest shoober on Instagram. He's thicc, humorous, and loves to let his presence be known with his famous "aroooos." He enjoys: a good scritch scratch, cold water, squishy balls, and—most importantly—chimkin nuggers!

I just think it's important to document that for the future.

The dog I was able to see was a basset hound named Dean the Basset Hound. To my surprise, everyone seemed very excited to be in the presence of Dean the Basset Hound, whose bio tells me that he is "the most famous Basset Hound in the world!" Incredulous, I approached three people in line to meet Dean whom I determined to be around my age but later realized were almost certainly at least a decade younger, ha-ha, oh god. I asked if they actually knew who this dog was. "Yes." "Yes." "Yes." They looked at me like I was insane.

Of course they knew who Dean was? *From Instagram?* Dean the Basset Hound? They were so mad at me for asking that they refused to even elaborate, and of course I was so sorry. (It's worth noting, too, that most of the people in line did not have their own dogs with them. Presumably they were there, at the festival, simply to meet Dean the Basset Hound.) I checked out his Instagram and found that three of my friends already followed him. I guess he is a celebrity. Huh. My mistake. Peter and I stood and watched him lounging on a chair in front of his audience for a few moments before leaving in shame. Our apologies to Dean.

Taking a last lap around the festival, we came across a gated-off area I'd walked by several times in the far corner of the park. It was generally empty, and I was under the impression that it was gated off because they didn't want dogs walking on the plush grass it protected. This time I noticed there were two dogs chasing each other inside, so Peter and I walked over to investigate. Two Woofstock representatives, sitting in an adjacent tent, approached us. "Oh good, someone wants to come in!"

The gated-off area was in fact a makeshift off-leash park. I let Peter free and he darted away, running wide, joyous circles with the other dogs in the soft grass. I stood there and watched him in the warm Woofstock sun.

Chapter 4

SHOULD MY DOG PLAY A SPORT?

I wish I assumed Peter was happy all the time. I'd love to be the type of person who could look at him lying on the couch and think, *Ah, to be a dog!* The type of person who might say something like, "Sleeping, eating, getting pet...gosh, Peter really has the life!" The type of person who sees their dog chewing on a bone and is able to think of anything other than the deep melancholy one must feel as a dog; trapped in this cruel human world, confused, alone, and made to watch *Gilmore Girls* with a regularity that is frankly inhumane.

Sigh.

I am clearly not that type of person, which is why it is such a relief that I have found something that makes Peter unmistakably, emphatically happy. Something that turns his little rubber tire frown upside down. Something that, for the love of god, isn't just lying on his side with his eyes open, staring lifelessly into nothingness.

And that something is—(take a pause, preparing to be shocked)—*recreational canine agility.*

Canine agility, the sport where dogs run through an obstacle course, pops into the American consciousness maybe once a year, around the time of the Westminster Kennel Club Dog Show. In 2019, you might recall, a bichon frise named Winky competed in the Masters Agility Championship Preliminaries there, and managed to capture the heart of the public when her run became popular on social media. There are two types of dogs who manage to capture the heart of the public this way: the ones who are very good at agility, and the ones who are very bad at agility. Winky, bless her, was the latter.

In her run, Winky takes her time with the course. Though speed is the goal, she is in no rush; she doesn't know when she'll be back at the Westminster Kennel Club Dog Show and she wants to take it all in. She moseys through the weave polls. She trots over the jumps. She enters the tunnel and, some time later, emerges from the other side. She pauses when she gets to the tippy top of the A-frame, looking out at her adoring fans, taking in their thunderous applause, far more interested in soaking up the moment than trying to beat the ticking clock. At the apex of the dog walk she takes another pause for more grandiose posing, more thunderous applause. She is regal. She is confident. She is a star.

She reminds me of Peter, in that way.

I was nearly certain Peter would be very good at agility. I suspect he has many secret talents he's kept hidden from me out of modesty, that's just the kind of guy he is, but I'd like him to know that it's okay to show off every once in a while— to paint a landscape, or speak out loud, or flawlessly complete a twelve-pole weave pole (the maximum pole amount used in canine agility competition). So off to Doggie Academy we went.

Doggie Academy is a semi-large dog obedience gym in the Park Slope section of Brooklyn, New York. It's not nearly as large as similar gyms in just about every other place in the country, but for the city it's pretty spacious. You can stretch out. Six people and their dogs can fit comfortably in a class, and there's enough room to practice smaller agility sequences: a few jumps, a tunnel. If you want to practice real agility runs, though, you'll have to work off-site. The floor is a padded blue foam, on which heels are specifically not allowed, and framed champion dog photos decorate the walls. I was happy to find that Doggie Academy offered classes in recreational canine agility, because Doggie Academy is not very far away from my apartment, and I love when things are close to my apartment.

Peter is very fast. He's a small guy, and his body wasn't necessarily built for speed—he looks like if a baby lamb swallowed a cannonball—but he makes do. He chases the faster guys around the park with aplomb; he runs away from me during our chase game (a game where I chase him) with an insulting intensity. I'd never seen him perform any stunts of standard agility, but I did once see him hip check a smaller dog right into a bush. The move was effortless; he tossed the dog with ease and kept on running. *O jogo bonito*, indeed.

I was unsure of how Peter would react to recreational canine agility, though, because I consider us to be one soul existing in two corporeal forms, and I was never, and am not currently, good at sports. I know I exude the confidence of someone notably good in a game of pickup basketball, but my inability to either dribble or even walk with conviction is likely more of a hindrance than an asset. I competed in a softball league at an old job, but this mainly consisted of drinking company-purchased beer and yelling insults at the other, typically less intoxicated teams. I was forced to be a cheerleader in grade school and, after showing up to several games in black tights and converse sneakers, was somehow mistakenly left off the call list by the mother in charge of coordinating the squad. This coincided with the discovery that I had scoliosis, a disease commonly used in sitcoms to denote a "nerd," and would need spinal fusion surgery and to wear a back brace for an entire year.

While I'd like to keep Peter as my special mini me forever, eagerly telling people that we are the same—for example, we were both born in Georgia, we're both a little shy, and in fact *our* favorite movie is *You Can Count on Me*—it was time to let him spread his wings. It was time to let him be his own dog. It was time to sign him up for Recreational Canine Agility I.

We were instructed to serve a lighter breakfast on our first class day, and to come with a lot of treats. I cooked Peter part of a chicken breast and half of a sweet potato, and mixed that in with his store-bought cookies, which to me felt like a normal thing to do—cost-effective and more exciting than usual—but which was immediately regarded as decadent and strange by my agility peers. "Wow . . . *fancy*," said Amanda, our young, candid, high school–teaching agility instructor. A withering comment, and not the last of its kind I'd receive.

At the beginning of class, we went around the group giving quick introductions. A large Russian man and his wife were taking the class with their chocolate Lab named Hershey. "I'm just a dick with a wallet!" the man said, to introduce himself to the class. It was as odd in the moment as it sounds now. We weren't *all* saying things like, "I'm just a dick with a wallet!" The rest of us were saying things like, "My name is Kelly and this is my dog, Peter." It was an interesting choice from what I assume is a fascinating man. Sadly, I did not get a chance to know him further. After this class, their teenage daughter, who was normal, took over Hershey's training.

We began training with a jump, which Amanda set up

relative to Peter's height. I'd never encountered one in real life before, and it was exhilarating to interact with something I'd previously only ever seen on TV. It was as if I were suddenly given the opportunity to sit on Chairy, or walk on Floory, or kiss Mark Ruffalo. Amanda told us to first lure our dogs over the jump with a treat, and then switch to tossing it out in front of them, so they're looking ahead and not at us. This would become necessary when they had multiple obstacles to tackle. Peter, undeterred by the fact that he'd never seen a jump like this in real life before (as far as I know), leapt over the object without hesitation. He was a natural and knew what to do innately, just like I would if given a chance with Mark Ruffalo.

With ease, he hopped over, again and again, propelled apparently by instinct and, no doubt, his love of "fancy" (ugh) treats. Later in class, we taught our dogs the command "target," which involved booping their noses to a blue circle on the floor after receiving the command: "Target!" Peter picked this up quickly, too. He'd jump and boop, jump and boop. Amanda explained that in agility, and dog training more generally, dogs don't get things wrong; they know what they're doing. The only thing that could possibly mess them up is their human teammate. Oh dear. Yes, I know what you're thinking. Things were not looking good for Peter.

I learned quickly that the hardest part was, indeed, my part. Everything I did communicated something to Peter— where I was pointing my toes, the way I was angling my hand as I waved him toward the obstacle, whether I was successfully hiding a treat in my palm—and, as Amanda pointed out, I was doing them all wrong. I would point my foot in the wrong direction and Peter would follow it. I would hold the treat in the incorrect hand and it would distract him. I would inelegantly wave my hand toward the tunnel, and that embarrassed us both. I had to perform each of these movements correctly and simultaneously, which required far more coordination than I was able to easily summon. I wanted to be a good teammate. But would my body allow it?

I thought it would be helpful to see agility teams competing in the flesh, so I looked for a nearby trial. Unsure about whether people typically attend small agility trials as spectators, I emailed in advance of attending one in Bay Shore, New York, on the South Shore of Long Island, to see if it was allowed. "Yes, if you aren't bringing a dog absolutely come and spectate!" a woman named Jess responded. "We'd love to have you."

I found upon arrival that, no—people don't typically attend small agility trials as spectators.

Inside the large Long Island gym, competitors stood with their dogs around a gated-off obstacle area with the standard blue foam floor. There were no seats. It was immediately clear that this trial was not meant to be taken in by anyone other than the competitors and the judges. In fact, I would have been the only spectator in attendance that day, but I was actually there on a third date. The other spectator was my date. (I'm including this not because it's any of your business, and please stop prying, but because I'd like to be honest about the number of spectators in attendance that day, which is two. I did not invite this man; I was explaining my upcoming plans to him and mentioned I had to drive out to Long Island for a dog agility trial and he said: "Can I come?" His name is Chris and he is, at the time of writing, my boyfriend. I will let you know if we break up, though again I have to stress that it isn't your business.)

We spotted some folding chairs along the wall and asked if we could grab them, and a helpful agility practitioner said yes. She told us we could set them up anywhere, which made sense, as everywhere seemed equally incorrect. We chose a place near the obstacle area's entrance gate. Every so often someone would come up to greet us. "Oh, you're the girl who emailed!"

To get a sense of the course before taking their dogs through it, the human half of the team is allowed a walk-through. This immediately became my favorite part. The humans jog through the course, fluttering their arms, lightly mimicking the movement they'll make during showtime. They run around the jumps, they spin, they call out to their invisible dogs. All the competitors do this at once. Though I'm admittedly not well versed in all the elements of sports, I have to imagine it is one of the odder elements of any sport. I love it.

And then the dogs come in. The main elements of this trial were a few jumps, weave poles, and a tunnel. They have to be completed in the correct order, quickly, and without error. The dogs seemed to have wild fun with this, and the spirit in the room that day was not at all competitive; everyone wanted each other to do well, and for the most part pretty much everyone did. A dalmatian sailed over the poles, a border collie barreled through the tunnel. This is, of course, save for a few rowdy outliers. Some dogs are just not meant to be tamed, and instead are meant to run around the course making an absolute fool out of the human who is attempting to get them to weave through multiple poles, an action that is not anywhere near the realm of what they are currently doing. At one point a bulldog, so pleased with his performance, jumped onto his human and began humping her. It pleased the room immensely.

After the standard agility runs, a woman approached us to politely ask something to the effect of what the hell we were doing there and why, and told us we were in for a treat—the next thing on the agenda was "snooker." I wish I'd recorded her explanation of snooker, because she explained it in only a few sentences, and every other explanation I've found takes up several pages. Suffice to say it is an agility game in which certain obstacles are worth a certain number of points, and other obstacles are worth another certain number of points, and you have to sort of . . . put together your own obstacles, hitting a certain number of each type of obstacle for, I guess, the most points...and...well...let's just say it's an agility game and don't worry about it.

The referee called out numbers I didn't understand while we watched dogs fly through the weave poles, over the jumps, and through the tunnel, each of their openmouthed faces fierce with glee. Some couldn't help but bark the entire time, as if their excitement had to escape through their mouths. Others would suddenly pause, as if they'd lost their train of thought, and refuse to continue, again making their owners look like absolute fools. It was wonderful. There should have been more spectators.

We moved on to larger obstacles in our second agility class. The six dogs would do them one by one while the class watched. While other dogs moseyed up to the obstacles unfazed, Peter was unable to mask his joy from the very moment I stood up from my folding chair, indicating that it was his time to do something. He whizzed around, spinning and spinning, hopping into the air, his mouth open wide, his eyes beaming. *It was his turn!* He was going to do...*something!* Not even the suggestion of dinner or a ride in the car could get him as excited as the suggestion of his turn in agility class. I feel it is my duty to tell you—just because it is a fact, and, again, I'm not in the business of lying—that he was the most charming dog in the class for this reason and everyone thought so.

We began with the tunnel. Amanda would hold the dogs at the entrance while the handler ran to the other end and then said, "Tunnel!," hopefully inspiring the dog to run to them. Each dog approached the tunnel gingerly; they were a bit reserved, understandably unsure about the large foreign tube they were being instructed to enter. Still, most of them ran through the tunnel when commanded. It took Peter a bit to understand that he was supposed to go through the tunnel and not around it, running to me sweetly and happy-faced doing the exact wrong thing, but his excitement never waned. After class he was thrilled and exhausted. I felt the kind of elation people claim exercise enables, though I wouldn't know firsthand.

Peter's first real issue in agility class came in week three, with a board meant to simulate the feeling of the seesaw obstacle. This was supposed to get him used to the texture, so that he'd have one fewer thing to acclimate to once he attempted the stunt, but he refused to so much as put a single paw on top of the board. What was this ruse that I was attempting to pull off? he wondered. Putting a treat on a scratchy board, attempting to lure him onto the trap...like he was some kind of fool! At first he would place one or two of his paws on the board before hopping off, and then he abandoned the idea entirely. It is important to set boundaries, I told him; he should consider this a strength rather than a weakness.

His primary issue in agility class, still, was me. In tunneling and performing a sequence of jumps, in the fourth class, my footing and hand movements became integral to the process.

Now it was about more than just evading Amanda's verbalized disappointment; I needed to lead him, tell him what to do, and keep his momentum up. Attempting to do this was deeply embarrassing. I would lead him into the jumps, thinking only about my feet, pointing like a wonky-footed duck to the right of the jump rather than toward it, while my incorrect arm waved vigorously, the treat in the wrong hand, while Peter just looked up at me, unsure of why he had been given such a hideously incompetent teammate. "You see what you did?" Amanda would say. "He was looking at you like, *what??* He would have done it, but your feet were pointed away from the jump!" I know. I know.

While Peter's elation and charm at having his turn at any obstacle only grew as the course continued—he was the star of the class, no doubt—it seemed, at times, like the other dogs might be outpacing him in technical skill. He would jump off the A-frame, when other dogs would stay on. He couldn't walk across the wobbly board. The other dogs would target with a seemingly greater ease, or complete a series of three jumps without ever pausing, while he got distracted between them. Hm. These other dogs must be professionals, I thought, sneaking in here and attempting to humiliate us with their years of hard-won skill. Their decades of learning. Their multiple past lives spent placing first in old-timey agility tournaments. These jerks! Who did they think they were fooling?

You should know they allow drinking at the Westminster Kennel Club agility tournament. I think this fact might help inform an accurate picture of it in your mind. Yes, the attendees are mostly the sort of people you would assume— quiet dog fans wearing T-shirts featuring pictures of specific breeds tucked into their jeans. But it's also a lot of people on "creative" dates, a lot of adults in hats with dog ears on them walking around with craft beers, and at least one guy who yelled, "YEAAAAAAAH! YOU GOT THIS!!!" at every competing dog. And me, there to see what could have been Peter's future if only he'd be born to another human mother, as well as a larger-scale and flashier version of my favorite sport: the freaky zombie ghost dog pre-competition walk-through. (It did not disappoint.)

You hear the "oooooohs" and "wwooooows" as soon as you enter the pier in which the tournament is located, which is the sort of wildly large echoey space typically used for things like trade shows. (The big breed judging competition takes place at Madison Square Garden, but the rest of it happens at these piers in Hell's Kitchen along the Hudson.) Dogs are everywhere, trotting around with their eyes dutifully trained on their owners. These dogs are alert. They are ready to compete. It was a decidedly different atmosphere from the Long Island trial, though an element they had in common was that there were no seats. Security guards ushered agility fans from one crowded area to another, telling them they weren't allowed to stand because people needed to get by and that they'd have to find a seat somewhere, even though the security guards knew as much as anyone this was an impossibility, there were no seats. The stands were packed with dog fans, gasping, cooing. That one guy yelling. Of course it was crowded, it was the agility event of the year.

I would compare my understanding of the Westminster Kennel Club's breed judging competition to my understanding of American football—I never know why anything is good or bad, or why points are given, or what is happening at all, until a winner is crowned. The agility competition, however, is more like basketball. Maybe I'm not getting the finer points, but I understand the gist: The ball goes in the hoop, the dogs who are the fastest and who visibly mess up the least are the ones who are doing the best. That ease of understanding makes the atmosphere during competition absolutely electric—you can tell most of those watching the competition only sort of know what's happening, but that they are, regardless, connected to it deeply. "OHHHH!" the crowd shouted when a dog mistakenly knocked over a jump pole. "HOLY SHIT!" the seemingly polite woman standing next to me said while Verb, a border collie and the 2019 Masters Agility Championship grand champion, was going through his run. I was familiar with Verb from his win the year before, and it was thrilling to see the star athlete compete right in front of me. He didn't win this time around (he came in fourth in the twenty-inch division), but his performance was stunning. Everyone in the audience was, correctly, freaking the fuck out about Verb.

The grand champion that day was a different border collie named P!nk, after the singer. (Border collies are preternaturally good at agility and had taken the grand champion title six out of the previous seven years.) P!nk has one brown eye and one blue eye, lending an air of madness to her otherwise composed demeanor. This intimidation technique combined with her skill had already won her first place in her division, the sixteen-inch class, two years in a row. Her run this year was just about flawless. She glided through the course with a cool intensity, letting out a single bark after every weave poll, slipping into moments of determined silence around her jumps.

After her run, an absolutely thrilled P!nk jumped right into her owner's arms, as if she knew she'd just won grand champion. Watching her happiness made me think of Peter. His joy. His skill. His undeniable charm. I just knew he had it in him to be... an *even more* grand champion.

There's a tricky element called the pause table inserted into agility courses that is meant to stop a dog's momentum; the dog has to leap onto the table and stand or sit there, still, for a designated amount of time before continuing onto their next obstacles. In class, we practiced the pause table only on its own, rather than as part of a sequence. Peter was the best in the class at pausing. This was a big win for him. He could hop up onto the table from any angle and, with the verbal command "wait" and the "stop" sign of my hand, he could wait there for just about any amount of time he needed to. While other dogs fidgeted, he was stoic. He could wait there all day. Then the verbal command "okay!" told him it was time to hop down again.

Pausing gave him confidence, and he hit his stride in our sixth and final class. Everything seemed to finally click. He was no longer afraid of the dog walk, and would rush fearlessly to boop the target I placed at the end. In a previous class he'd gotten used to the seesaw by putting one paw on it and pressing it down, then getting a treat. Then putting two paws on it and pressing it down, then getting a treat. Then getting a treat with every step he took onto the obstacle, coaxing him through the object's fall. Now he barely needed more than one treat to complete the seesaw in its entirety.

Peter didn't seem to mind that I hadn't progressed as much as a teammate. I mostly stopped caring, too. He was happy with my terrible job even when it lead him astray, because it still led him to his "fancy" (ugh) treats, and it still led him to fun. It seems unlikely that he'll enter into competitions, but we've accepted that as a team. It's enough just to know that he *could* be a champion, better and faster and more agile than any dog has ever been in history—if only it weren't for me.

Chapter 5

SHOULD I BUY MY DOG A BUNCH OF STUFF HE DOESN'T NEED?

My most regrettable Peter-related purchase is a $60 handmade dog-size re-creation of the knitted Apollo sweater Danny Torrance wears in *The Shining*. I know what you're thinking: But a $60 handmade dog-size re-creation of the knitted Apollo sweater Danny Torrance wears in *The Shining* sounds incredible. And you're right, it is. But—I'll explain.

It was our second Halloween together, and while I didn't want Peter to suffer the indignity and panic that a dog costume would provide—something like a hot dog, or dinosaur, or pope—we were going to be handing out candy together, and I thought it would be nice if he was a little festive. A little spooky. Warm in a sweater, but a famous sweater, a *cool* sweater—a sweater from one of my favorite movies, *The Shining*, which admittedly he has never seen, but which I think he would like if he had the capacity to like human movies and was not appropriately afraid of men yelling.

That I was able to instantly find someone online to create for me a dog-size version of the sweater Danny Torrance wears in *The Shining* is, I think, part of what many would call "the problem." But at the time it felt like it was meant to be. Finally, something good had come out of Al Gore's despicable internet. I hate to even consider the highest amount I would have paid for the sweater, but I suppose for the sake of honesty I should tell you I would have likely gone up to $100. I'm sorry. Unlike Peter and *The Shining*, I am imperfect. "Luckily," though, it was "only," as I said, $60.

I bought the sweater well in advance and eagerly awaited its arrival. *This will be perfect*, I thought. *Yes, it will be extra perfect for Halloween, but this is something he'll be able to wear all winter. This is something to treasure for years to come!* For him, it would just be a sweater he disliked that would warm him on cold walks, but for me it would be... Well, it would be a sweater that reminded me of a movie. Admittedly it doesn't sound that impressive when written out, but maybe someone outside would see him in the sweater and think to themselves, *Huh, the sweater on that dog is like the sweater from that movie*. And you have to admit—that recognition would be priceless.

The sweater arrived eventually and I was elated and then immediately disappointed. It was too large, which is my fault. I'm not very good at measuring Peter. I think for this piece of clothing I sort of tried to measure him using a tape measure and...I don't know. I really dislike numbers, and having to look at them, and I'm pretty sure a tape measure is not the correct way to measure a dog, so I pretty much just guessed, and I'd like you to leave me alone.

Plus (I'm not done) dog size in general is just difficult. There is no uniform system. Medium? Small? Large? You never know what your dog is until you order something and it's wrong. To me, Peter is so tiny that sometimes I can barely even see him, but a lot of the time his dog size will (allegedly, according to weight) be either "Large" or "Extra Large." Excuse me? Once a company asked for the circumference of Peter's neck and I looked up how to measure circumference and the answer was "π x the diameter of the circle," and I'm sorry but no, I'm not doing that, are you fucking kidding me, I absolutely do not know how to, so I said "just give me a medium," and they did. And it was too large!

I forget what I was talking about. Oh. Yes, so the sweater was too big, but not so big that he couldn't wear it, just big enough that it looked too big and not quite as handsome as I imagined. I thought that might be nice, though; a larger sweater might feel more comfortable for him, less like he was being threatened by fabric at all times.

He was immediately afraid of the sweater. It reminded me of the time I spent almost $100 on the materials necessary to build a dog gingerbread house for him that he could fit inside of for Christmas, but which he would not enter due to fear, which reminds me that *that* was actually my most regrettable Peter-related purchase, due not only to the expense but also to the fact that baking all the dog-friendly gingerbread and building the structure and applying the pieces took several weeks. The sweater is number two.

The sight of it frightened him. He knew exactly what it was. Clothes, dreaded clothes. He's like this with his winter coat, too, which he wears during snow. When it's coaty time he sits by the door, ears plastered against his skull, seemingly attempting to make himself invisible; if only he could disappear, then perhaps he wouldn't have to wear the little coat. I can always still see him, though, much to his sadness. I apologized and put the sweater on him, to see if he might be less afraid once he realized it was an expensive novelty item his caretaker had mistakenly purchased for him because she is bad with money, and that she needed him to at least be okay with it in order to prevent a shame spiral. He wandered around with it on inside of my apartment, suspiciously.

We went out for a walk, during which I snapped a photo—the lone photo of him in the Danny sweater. He is near a tree, looking back at me with unhappy ears and a face that says, unmistakably, *Are you fucking kidding me with this?* It says, *You know I hate this sweater and now you're parading me around in it, AND you're taking a fucking photo?* I cut our walk short, ashamed.

Back inside, he hopped on top of our bed with it before disappearing under the covers. His form shifted underneath the comforter and it looked as if the bed were giving birth to a large fish. Something was occurring, clearly. He was solving a problem under there. A few moments later he finally emerged—fully nude. It was astonishing. "How did you do that?" I asked, but of course an angry magician never reveals the tricks he was forced to perform under duress. My poor, sweet Houdini. I never attempted the sweater again.

According to a survey from the American Pet Products Association that you've likely come across if you've ever read an article about any sort of dog product, humans in the US spent an estimated $75 billion on their pets in the year 2019. This is up a bit from the paltry $72 billion they spent the year before. For context, according to the same survey, about 85 million families in the US (67 percent of households) own a pet, which makes the amount spent per family the result of $75 billion divided by 85 million. You may do the calculation yourself if you are so inclined; you already know how I feel about math.

I think most people hear $75 billion and imagine dogs living in luxury with bedazzled collars and tufted beds, or little doggy mansions with a doggy swimming pool and doggy recessed lighting and reclaimed doggy subway tile, but it might comfort you to know that most of that amount ($32 billion) goes to food. Then vet care and pet insurance ($19 billion), then medicine ($16 billion), and the actual purchasing of animals ($2 billion). The rest, about $6 billion, goes to things like grooming, training, pet sitting, and toys.

Six billion is still a lot of billions, I'm sure you're thinking, and it's true. *Even if the entire amount were just $6 billion, I would still think it was a lot.* Yeah, I know. *Like, $6 billion is probably even more than the US spends on education in a year*, you're thinking, and no, it's not, but I get what you're saying and I urge you to relax.

Something you're really gonna hate, though, especially as it relates to my earlier story, is that the National Retail Federation estimates that $480 million of the $72 billion spent on pets in 2018 was spent on pet Halloween costumes. This is double the amount that was spent on pet Halloween costumes in 2010, when the NRF began tracking the number. I imagine this is due to the rise of social media, and people sharing their pets in costumes online. "Like" if you think my dog looks like an astronaut. "Fav" if you think my cat looks like Mr. Bean. "Share" if you think your followers might enjoy a herd of rabbits dressed as the cast of *Friends*.

It's a plainly horrifying number, mostly because any large amount of money tied to a frivolous expenditure evokes the number of people and animals who could be helped by that amount of money if it were spent on charity rather than useless personal goods. But it's also horrifying for the simple fact that pets hate Halloween costumes. Hundreds of millions of dollars spent to make our pets dislike us a little more than they already do. Hundreds of millions of dollars to make them, the innocent creatures in our care, needlessly uncomfortable. Hundreds of millions of dollars for a *Shining*-related sweater that is just going to be in my drawer now forever, until I no doubt one day attempt to put it on a human baby. It is perhaps not the best use of hundreds of millions of dollars.

This sort of spending, we can at least say definitively, is useless. It's less obvious to me, though, whether we should be buying the other stuff. The plush toys, the supposedly mind-stimulating dog puzzles. The monthly subscription boxes full of treats and toys. The first thing I ever bought for Peter was a three-pack of bones, one that was fully edible and two that were just for chewing. I know it sounds like an impersonal gift, and you can trust that it was even more impersonal than it sounds; I picked them out after I signed up to be a foster, intending them to be for whatever dog I was assigned. I once read an interview with Drake where he said he owns shelves and shelves of Birkin bags he's collected as a gift for whomever his future wife turns out to be. A bit odd, but I understand. It reminded me of when I bought the bones. Luckily Peter was unable to ascertain that they were bought only to please the general idea of a dog. And they did seem like a good gift. A bone is a classic dog accoutrement, and this three-pack had a little variety. One of them was an opaque white, to trick the dog into thinking his good fortune had potentially led him to a real bone. Another was inexplicably blue and bumpy. *Let's make this one...blue and bumpy*, you can imagine the dog product developer saying, and you better believe they did it. The edible one was brown.

Along with the bones, I bought a dog bed and some kibble. I remember watching him the first night we were in my apartment together, as he was resting in the dog bed, chewing on the white bone. I didn't even have to explain them to him. He just got in the dog bed, picked up the bone with his mouth, held it in his paws, and chewed on it. I took a picture of him and sent it to my friends. *"He's in his dog bed!!!! And he's CHEWING on the BONE!!!!"* It felt good to be able to provide that bit of comfort and pleasure for him in what was undoubtedly a confusing and difficult time. The gifts seemed to do him some good.

Now that I know him, though, my yearnings for what I'd like to provide for him have gotten more precise. I still buy him chew toys, and stuffed things, and beds, and everything else, but I'd really like to buy him something big. Something life-changing. What I'd *really* like to buy Peter is a laptop. I'll give you a moment to imagine it. Doesn't that sound like the kind of gift he deserves? Expensive, solid, able to compute things. A laptop is a statement gift, a real "leveling-up" sort of purchase. It's fun, but useful—you can surf the internet, or put together a spreadsheet. It would be an investment in his future. I think about how much I'd like to buy him a laptop with what one might deem an alarming frequency.

But what kind of laptop can you buy a dog? A stuffed laptop, probably. Or maybe a fake little plastic laptop that you put in front of him for a photo that you caption something like: "Buster is helping me out at work today, LOL."

Insulting. A laptop—a *real* one—would be exciting. It would be impressive. He would know how much I loved him, if I could buy him a laptop. That's the kind of gift I'd like to get him.

But of course I can't buy him a laptop, because a laptop is not for dogs. The options for actual dog-related gifts are at once stupefyingly outrageous and remarkably boring. Even the really expensive things aren't particularly thrilling: doghouses that cost thousands of dollars, dog-size dresses decorated with actual diamonds. The internet is rife with lists like "26 Things You Won't Believe You Can Buy Your Dog," and it's all, like, a dog bed shaped like a hamburger, or "dog beer." Who wants that? It's useless. There just isn't enough exciting, usable innovation in the dog product arena.

Still, I'm not sure that means we should be ashamed of the money we spend on our small friends. When people come into my apartment and take note of Peter's disgusting toy mound, they usually remark that he is quite a lucky dog to have so much stuff, the subtext of which is that I am a fool to have spent so much money on this filthy mound of chewed-up trash. I like to point out, though, that the rest of the stuff in the apartment is mine. He only has the one disgusting mound. Why shouldn't he?

But I admit there have been missteps. Out of honesty, here is a condensed list of what Peter has had to deal with in terms of dog products purchased by myself or given to him otherwise:

PUZZLE TOY

This was one of those toys where you put treats into different hidden sections on a plastic board, and the dog has to figure out how to manipulate the board in order to find the treats. A horrible convoluted task. Peter hated this puzzle toy and so did I. He didn't see pawing at a board for the hope of a tiny piece of sustenance while humans watch for their own entertainment as a good use of his time, and I can't see why any dog would. Stupid puzzle. It's insane to me that anyone takes pleasure in doing any sort of puzzle, either of the human or dog variety. Once I attempted to do a puzzle while on vacation at a cabin and I got about as far as dumping the pieces out of the box before I realized what a sham it all is. Putting together a thousand pieces of something that came to you broken, without being paid for your effort. Why? I regret buying him the puzzle toy and putting any money into the puzzle market in general.

HIDDEN TREAT BALL TOY

A ball with a hole in which you are meant to stuff treats for the dog to figure out how to release. Essentially another puzzle. What we—the dog-item-buying public—are hoping for with these sort of "smart" toys is that the dogs can find a way to amuse themselves for a period of time, expand their minds, and make us feel less guilty for not being able to play with them the amount they'd like to be played with. Unfortunately life is not about buying away your guilt; it's about holding your guilt on your back until it crushes you. A puzzle toy isn't going to change that.

LARGE BALL THAT MADE A NOISE WHEN IT MOVED

I'm not sure why I thought he would like this. I bought it as a Christmas gift, in a jumble of other Christmas gifts, hoping, I think, that Peter would at least be impressed by the quantity of gifts if not the quality. But I should've chosen this gift more thoughtfully. The ball was too big for him, and the plastic was hard, and it made this sound: *meeeuooop!* I'm not sure why any dog would like that. Why did they make this toy and for whom? I can only shoulder part of the blame; the other part lies with the manufacturer. The ball exists in my parents' backyard now and sometimes, when we're back there, I'll kick it for him. He does not chase it.

PLUSH PLATYPUS

A friend bought Peter a plush platypus as an adoption gift, and he loved it dearly. He would cuddle with it when we watched movies together, or thrash it around in his mouth. And he would never attempt to disembowel it, even though every dog knows disemboweling is the most thrilling part of any plush toy. He kept his friend the platypus intact for about a year and a half. I'm not sure what happened between them at that point, but it was then that Peter decided the platypus had to die. Finally, he took the fabric flesh into his maw and yanked out the innards. For a while after that I'd stuff the filthy guts back in the platypus so Peter could disembowel him again and again, but it soon became clear that it was time for a new platypus. We'd lost a good amount of the guts. He doesn't like the new one as much. It is perhaps my fault for thinking the platypus could be replaced, or that the rift between them, whatever it was, could be mended so easily.

KONG

The Kong is essentially a non-puzzle delivery mechanism for treats, and as such Peter loves it. Peter is not, however, particularly good at getting all the treats out of the Kong before abandoning it. This is maybe due to my peanut butter–layering technique. A layer of peanut butter, a layer of kibble, a layer of peanut butter, a layer of kibble, frozen in the freezer. I found out he couldn't really empty it after taking his discarded Kong and placing it on my bedside table, next to my bedroom window. Shortly after I noticed there was a shimmering conga line (Kong-a line) going from my window to inside of the Kong. How very interesting. Upon closer inspection it seemed to be, yes, an enormous line of ants, leading to, ah yes, a Kong absolutely filled to the brim with ants. That was my fault.

KONG BEAR

The Kong bears with rope skeleton innards are filthy, disgusting pleasures, and Peter absolutely loves them. They hang around his toy pile with their guts all hanging out, ropy and mangled and gruesome, faces torn half off, just begging guests to question my ability to discern when something is ready to be thrown out. It is my great pleasure both to provide Peter with endless new skeleton bears to maim, and to keep the old ones as a warning.

PHALLIC-LOOKING ITEM THAT WAS SUPPOSED TO HELP CLEAN HIS TEETH

This penis item is a lie. I'm not sure how it could clean teeth the way it claims to. It's like a big green…well, penis, like I said, with little rubber hairs on its shaft. You put the doggy toothpaste inside of the hairs, and your dog is supposed to chew on it, as if he were chewing on a very large toothbrush, and brush his own teeth. Yeah right. I highly doubt this has ever happened with any dog. Peter at first ignored the green penis and then licked out all of its toothpaste, which I can't imagine served any sort of oral-hygiene-related purpose and which was frankly disturbing to behold.

FANCY DOG BED

When I sold this book I wanted to buy Peter something really good, but I couldn't come up with anything, because all I could think about was buying him a laptop, and I KNOW, you don't need to tell me, we've already gone over it, I can't buy him a laptop. So I got a few different normal toys and treats, and this fancier-than-normal dog bed. It doesn't exactly look "fancy," it looks sort of like a small, bare mattress, but it also *feels* like a small, bare mattress, and therein lies the fanciness. It's at once plush and sturdy, like for a human. I've yet to come across any small doggy sheets, but you know I'd buy them if I did. He sleeps in my bed at night, so this is just for day lounging. He sometimes goes on it.

DOG WINE

A friend gave me this. Part of me wishes I could understand its existence but a larger part is glad my mind can't reach the depths of depravity necessary to do so. Dog wine, why? Are you feeding this to your dog? Are you alone drinking and you give the dog "wine," too, in a cup? Please don't. It's okay to just drink wine by yourself. I wouldn't advise that you drink a lot of wine by yourself, but ultimately I'm not going to police your wine intake. Life can get stressful. I am going to police your dog's "wine" intake, however, and tell you that he can have absolutely: NONE!

ABSOLUTELY ADORABLE RAIN BOOTIES

The devil's booties, will not keep them on for a single second.

HANDHELD BALL LAUNCHER

There are many options out there for the non-city-dwelling dog owner who wants to scare her dog in the backyard with an automatic ball launcher, but those of us in the city are mostly relegated to the handheld kind. I didn't really think Peter would be into this type of toy, because he became easily bored when I'd throw the ball for him with my hand, always running after it only a few times before abandoning the activity in search of urine to smell. But one day Chris, my boyfriend, offered to toss him a ball from his ball launcher while we both had our dogs (his dog's name is Frank) at the park.

First, Chris offered that I try it myself. But a problem I have with the ball launcher is that it seems to be broken whenever I attempt to use it. It pitches the ball directly into the dirt, rather than allowing the ball to hurdle far out into the field like when everyone else uses it. A factory defect. So, Chris offered to pitch the ball for Peter with the ball launcher and, to my absolute disbelief, Peter went *chasing after it*, and then *retrieved it in his mouth*, and then *brought it back to us and then dropped it on the ground*. He did this several times in a row. We only stopped because it was time to go, not because he ever got sick of it. It was completely disillusioning. Who was this dog? Who was this beloved stranger?

Sadly I cannot duplicate this experience for Peter myself due to the ball launcher's error, but it is thrilling to know that this other dog exists inside of him somewhere. We can still surprise each other, yet.

SQUIRRELS IN A LOG TOY

I bought this toy because every dog owner I've ever known on earth made a point to tell me it was good, and my rebellious nature regrets to inform you that they were all correct. The "log" has several holes in it, through which your dog can delight in pulling out plush squirrels before tossing them around and eventually destroying them. If you're willing, you can even put your hand into the log, grab onto a squirrel, and give your dog a harder time pulling him out. *"Ooh, you'll never get mee!"* you can say in a squirrel voice. *"Ohh, Peter! Peter! I dare you to get me! You can't! You can't!" "Oohh no, Peter! Peter, you're killing me, nooo!"*

HEATHER-GRAY SHERPA THROW BLANKET THAT I BOUGHT FOR MYSELF

I bought this blanket in a store that is typically too expensive for me to buy anything in. It was on sale, though, and it was remarkably soft, and if you remember I am not good with money. Peter agreed that it was something special, and sat on it with all of his might as soon as I put it down on the couch. He'd lie on it, burrow underneath it, sit immovably upon it whenever an opportunity presented itself. He enjoyed the blanket so much that without much effort on his part, it became his. "Do you want your blanket?" I'd ask him, about my blanket. "Let me get you your blanket."

DOG PLUSH TOY A FRIEND HAD PURCHASED FOR ME

Before I fostered Peter, I was briefly under the impression that I was going to adopt a different dog. He was a white Bedlington-terrier-looking little guy, and I walked him every day for a few weeks at Sean Casey Animal Rescue, the dog shelter down the street from where I lived. When he walked on a leash, always slowly, he would periodically pause and look back at me, seemingly to make sure I was still there. It just killed me. He was found on the street and brought in, and was going to be available for adoption once some amount of time had elapsed, giving his owners a chance to come and claim him if they were going to do so. So I would come in and walk him every day and ask if I could adopt him yet.

One day I came by and he wasn't there anymore. I asked for him, and was told his owners had come to get him. I was devastated, but I understood. He was back with his owners and he was theirs, not mine. Later on the shelter's Instagram page, I saw my little dog in the arms of another woman, with a caption that announced he'd just been—hold on, excuse me: ADOPTED? I called the shelter to see what the fuck. They said this other woman had been coming in to walk him every day, and asked each time about adopting him, until the answer was yes. No, I thought, that was ME DOING THAT! I couldn't believe it. While part of me believed that there had been some sort of error, that she'd swooped in and stolen the dog that was rightfully mine, I guess it's more likely that both of us were there walking him every day, fantasizing about our futures with the little white dog, thinking we were the only one. Luckily for both of us, her timing was better.

To soothe me, my friend Leah sent me a small stuffed dog along with a note about how I'd someday find the dog I was meant to have. In his first few days of living at my apartment, Peter completely destroyed it.

CHAPTER 5.5: DESCRIPTIONS OF PETER'S VARIOUS PLUSH TOY–RELATED GAMES

1. "THAT'S MY TURTLE!"

In this game the turtle is mine. He's a sea turtle and he is pristine—Peter cannot have him. I circle the turtle around Peter's snout; a ruse. I toss him ahead of me knowing full well Peter will bring him right back; fool. He can never have the turtle. It's my turtle. And wait—what's that? The turtle seems to be ringing. It seems the turtle is a phone. I bring the turtle to my head, *"Hello? You'd like to talk to Peter? Peter the dog? Yeah, he's right here, I'll get him, one second."* It's for you, Peter. It's the turtle. And he's mine.

2. "THAT'S MY DUCK!"

Admittedly this game is played with his platypus toy. No matter. The duck is mine. Peter pounces on the duck's ragged body as I drag the low-stuffed corpse across the carpet. He'll never get him. He can pounce and bite and attempt to grab the duck, but the duck is mine. I hold the duck in front of his face, and as soon as he chomps I pull it away, throwing his head to the right and to the left, telling him, "THAT'S MY DUCK." And it is.

3. "THAT'S MY DONUT!"

Oh, could there be anything as humiliating as a donut on the snout? Here you were, attempting to grab my cloth donut now entirely drained of its former plush, and not only were you denied, but now it is placed at once so close and so hideously out of reach. That is what you get when you attempt to snatch *my* donut.

4. "THAT'S MY GUY!"

We don't always know what these sort of guys are supposed to be. I think one of them is a Viking. Another is maybe a moose. One of them is certainly Gumby. Regardless, they're my guys. My guy thrown across the room for you to fetch for me. My guy dangling just out of reach. Hop to your feet, I dare you; it will do you no good. Oh, Peter, you cannot have the guy—he is mine.

Chapter 6

SHOULD I SPY ON MY DOG?

I love watching Peter.

I love watching him while he's eating his breakfast, chomping on his kibble with his loudest possible chomp. While he's sitting next to me with his butt on a pillow looking intensely at something I can't see, which I presume to be a ghost. While he's choosing a toy to gnaw on from his disgusting toy mound. While he's sleeping, his belly rising and falling so sweetly, either puppy barking in a dream or just lying still until I accidentally wake him up by shouting "I LOVE YOU!" While he's sitting at the door, wondering why I'm staring at him with eyes teary at his stoic beauty, instead of just please taking him for a walk. While he's pounding his front paws on the ground and thrashing his body around upon my return home, seemingly unable to control his indomitable joy, though I do understand that reading of the situation is a little conceited. While he's sniffing a single leaf for a very long time. While he's paused, one paw up, catching a scent in the air like a tiny detective. While he's circling around and around on the couch trying to find the perfect place to plop his cannonball body. While he's lying on my bed with open eyes, staring vacantly into space, seemingly wondering where it all went wrong. I absolutely love it. I could watch him all day.

And I do.

The idea to turn my apartment into a surveillance state came while I was getting a manicure. The salon was sterile and quiet. I'd chosen a deep purple to telegraph my dignity and mental fortitude, and while my manicurist was applying the polish I was suddenly overcome with the idea that Peter was dead. Or dying. Or injured. Or kidnapped! It was one of those knowing feelings that are right just often enough that you tend to believe them; when you're suddenly aware that something…is wrong. Something has happened.

Admittedly, I'd had this feeling a lot since adopting Peter, pretty much every time I was not looking directly at him. It was never correct. He was never dead. The apartment had never caught on fire, the window-unit air conditioner had never somehow fallen inside of my window at a moment when he was standing directly beneath it, he'd never stumbled upon some errant grapes or chocolate or garlic. He'd never fallen off my bed and broken all of his limbs, a lightbulb never burst to cover him and the floor with broken glass. He never suddenly stopped breathing. He never suffocated underneath a blanket. He never jumped out of a window because he saw a bird or a squirrel. He was never kidnapped by an obsessive neighbor with good taste.

(All real fears.)

Still, the *something has happened* feeling felt real every time. And it's hard to convince yourself that what you're feeling is unjustified, even if what you're feeling, regarding your air conditioner in particular, defies both common sense and physics. I didn't leave the nail salon prematurely that day (I'm very brave), but I did decide that something had to be done. "Therapy and pharmaceuticals," you're hoping, but no. Smartphone-based spying.

A few months before my panicked manicure, my friend Allie had given me an Amazon Cloud Cam that I, afraid of both the prying eyes of Jeff Bezos and the process of "setting up" a "device," had yet to put to use. Her then-boyfriend Adam (they're engaged now) (I want you to have the most up-to-date information) had tested out a bunch of home security cameras for work (he's a tech writer) (let me know if you want to know anything else about Allie and Adam), so they had a surplus. They used one to spy on their dog, and Allie thought I might want to spy on Peter, too. Thank you, Allie.

Unlike something like the "Furbo," which is a camera that allows you to drone-strike treats at your dog while watching him from afar, the Amazon Cloud Cam is not strictly geared toward dog-based spying. It is just one of many options in home surveillance, each offering some degree of scariness and artificial intelligence, and all able to be viewed on your phone. Mine is not particularly intelligent, as far as I know. For example, unlike some other cameras, it can't tell you specifically which people are passing in front of it, or where in the room they are passing. It can't say, "ALERT: YOUR BOY-FRIEND IS ON THE LEFT." Or, "ALERT: YOU'RE IN THE ROOM NOW, TOO." Or, "ALERT: BE CAREFUL BY THE BOOKCASE, YOU DIDN'T ANCHOR IT TO THE WALL." It can only alert you to the fact that something is happening somewhere. I was able to set it to turn off when my phone is connected to my Wi-Fi and turn on when my phone isn't, though, which I enjoy. And it captures videos when it senses movement, for however long the movement lasts. I also enjoy that, as it allows me to watch Peter stretch if I happen to miss it.

Now I watch Peter constantly. While I'm on the train, while I'm at work, while I'm at a bar, while I'm in a restaurant. I check in many times per outing. I make sure he's alive, not crying, limbs intact; I zoom in on his belly and make sure he's breathing. I show my phone to a friend and ask, "Do you think he's breathing?" And they say, "Yes, he's breathing." I don't trust their quick response so I zoom back in on his belly and see the pixels are moving, but think that could be due to shifting light. I look until he takes a deep breath and I can be absolutely sure that he's alive. Then I can look away for a few minutes.

Every time I check in he is always doing the same thing, which is nothing. He's just lying there, maybe in a slightly different position than the last time I checked. It's painful, really. If you're not watching your dog on a livestream it's easy to imagine he's doing something fun—reading, watching TV, tidying up in a pleasant little way. Making a snack. Maybe playing a video game, if you keep them in the house. Practicing a hobby. But he isn't. What he's doing, at least in Peter's case, is sleeping. Waiting around for me to come back. Lying with his eyes open. Standing up to rearrange himself, then plopping back down. I would understand if you abstained from getting a pet camera simply to avoid confronting the reality of your dog's boring days.

My friend Leah abandoned her pet camera for this reason, in fact. She found it made her more sad to have the ability to watch her dog, a Brussels griffon named Baby, just sitting there waiting for her to come home than it did to live her life outside of the apartment without the possibility. Would this be the right decision for me, too? I wonder about the healthfulness of my spying while I wait for movies to end, my heart racing, thinking about how I'm going to pull up my dog camera as soon as the credits roll to find Peter has died. I consider what, exactly, I'm gaining when I almost leave Super Bowl parties because I can't see him on the camera and convince myself that he fell out of the window. I question my choice when I prop up the camera behind my beer at a bar and then one of my co-workers comes into the bar and sees me doing it and she mentions it to me first thing on Monday.

Should I stop?

I don't even know for sure if the camera is really useful. If I checked in and my apartment was on fire and I was at the office, forty-five minutes away, what would I do? Call a neighbor and call my landlord and call a friend who lives close by who has a copy of my keys and tell them all my dog is inside my on-fire apartment and he needs to get out immediately? Yes. Okay. Well, solved that one. But what if I checked in and he was choking? If I checked in and he wasn't, in fact, breathing? If I checked in and he *had* jumped out the window, maybe to catch a squirrel? Is there much practical application in terms of dog safety, or am I checking in only to give myself a false sense of control in a situation over which I have very little agency?

"People can maybe overread some things. Like, if your dog, for example, had trouble jumping up on the couch once and you saw it on camera, but he jumped up on the couch normally nine other times..." I talked to Carly Fox, a staff doctor at New York City's Animal Medical Center, to see if there might be a practical reason for the spying. She said that watching can lead to overthinking; nervously reading a problem into a harmless situation, like maybe that your dog had fallen into a sinkhole that opened up in your apartment floor somehow and now he's trapped with the skeleton of an old coal miner, when really he'd just briefly walked out of the camera's range.

A dog with a known medical condition is different, however—like a dog with a history of seizures. "I think it is actually really useful for dogs that have a condition that requires monitoring," Fox said. This makes sense; then, you could monitor them. Admittedly Peter does not have a condition like this. It seemed there wasn't a particularly good health-related reason for my ceaseless spying. As far as other practical applications, she mentioned that if you happened to catch a collapse episode or a weird neurologic thing and your camera maintains video recordings, the video evidence would be useful. "It helps with a diagnosis—to see if it's oh, that was nothing, or, oh we should investigate that a little more." And, yes, I do suspect this will be the government's excuse as well.

I do wonder if I, too, am being monitored on the camera. I keep a piece of paper taped to the front-facing laptop camera for this reason: in case of spying. A vague fear of hacking. Mark Zuckerberg does the same thing, and you can bet he knows a lot about unsolicited surveillance. I guess I just have to accept that it's a possibility, that a group of hackers could be out there watching me eat dinner, watching me fold the couch blanket, watching me watch Peter.

I wonder if my hackers love watching him, too.

It's lucky that, presumably unlike the government, we don't really have the option to keep an eye on everyone all day long. If you knew you could do it, it would be tempting. "Let me just check in on the Leah cam…make sure she didn't die…"

I think the fear would be more present in your mind if you knew you could have that release.

"You're raising, like, the fundamental dilemma, right? What is the thing that is going to make me feel comforted? Is it knowing, or is it being able to distance myself and have some separation?" I talked to Kelly Scott (we have the same first name) over the phone. She's a therapist at Tribeca Therapy in New York City. "If there are actual logistical needs, reasons to keep your eye on the situation so you can respond if needed, I think that makes a ton of sense," she said. "But I think that when it comes to, like, 'I just feel so anxious being separated from my pet that I need to maintain that connection,' I think it's potentially more harmful than helpful."

It's difficult to monitor and think objectively about your own behavior; to note yourself doing something without actively knowing that you're doing it and that it will end up being noted. Still, I wanted to spend a day tracking all of my check-ins. Because of the difficulty of self-monitoring, this would have ideally been done by hiring a private eye to spy on me, but apparently many of them require some sort of retainer, starting at around $1,500, and I just don't have that kind of cash to spend on this project, not that I'm not dedicated to it.

So I chose to monitor myself, and I chose a day when I had to leave my home to go into the dreaded office for a meeting. I severely dislike going into the office. Mostly because I have to leave Peter, but also because I just find it very difficult to work in a fluorescently lit space where at any moment someone can walk up behind you and force you to introduce yourself to a new co-worker while everyone around you pretends not to listen to the interaction, even though the office is deadly silent and everyone can hear everything. *Hey, um. Welcome! It's, ah...are you excited to um, work here?*

I took notes in the notes app on my phone.

1:04 p.m.: Check-in from subway stop while waiting for train. Peter awake and lying down with head up, looking.

1:20 p.m.: Check-in from platform during train transfer. Peter awake and lying down with head down.

1:42 p.m.: Check-in from desk. Peter asleep and lying down with head down.

2:30 p.m.: Check-in from desk. Peter facing opposite direction. Can see only ears. Body obscured by blanket.

I was planning on entertaining you with all of it, but suffice to say it goes on like this. I checked in thirteen times in a five-hour period, though whether this is an accurate display of how often I would have checked had I not been monitoring myself is of course unclear. My final check-in was on the walk from the subway back to my apartment, where I caught Peter in the same position he'd been in the previous two times I'd checked.

Why am I doing this? I thought about it. My main fear is that Peter is going to suddenly die. The fears that follow that are that his death will be because of something I did or didn't do, that I'm going to be alone, that I will never be able to feel anything other than sadness from that point forward, but sudden death is the main fear. From what I could tell, much of the time remembering the existence of the camera preceded the fear. *I should check in on Peter—DID HE DIE? What app should I look at...oh yes, why not camera app...oh no—IS HE DEAD?* The camera was squelching a fear, but one that only seemed to exist so loudly because of the camera.

"If you're able to keep it more for...you're sitting at your desk, and you're overcome by this worry and this anxiety"—this is Kelly Scott, the therapist, again—"and you're like, oh my god let's see if my dog's okay, and you're able to look at the camera and see, oh yeah, he's chewing on a ball, he's fine..."—she thinks this is okay. But it becomes a problem when it becomes a distraction; that is, "when it's no longer something that soothes a concern, when you can't put it away and move on with your day."

Scott compared it to a relationship. A check-in every once in a while is fine, but constant worrying, constant checking in, constant, *are we okay? are you okay? are you mad at me? are you upset?* This is not good.

I tried to forget about the camera on a recent outing. I think it will take some time. I like being able to check on Peter, I like being able to see him. I like being able to show his live feed to friends. I like being able to see his belly rise and fall and feel, at least for that moment, at ease. But I'm trying to trust he's fine without having to see it. That he hasn't been crushed by the window-unit air conditioner. That he hasn't been kidnapped, or fallen into some crater-like situation. Am I succeeding? Well. I'm not looking at the camera *right now*, so.

Chapter 7

SHOULD I SLEEP IN BED WITH MY DOG?

It's funny to think back to a time when I thought I valued any possession more than Peter's freedom to destroy it. When I first took him in as a foster, I was under the impression that he would not sleep in my bed. It was against the rescue's rules, first of all, but I'd also recently purchased a linen duvet cover that cost $169, and that was on sale and with a discount code. I loved it very much. The duvet cover was beautiful—soft, pristine, and a soothing pastel pink, the exact color of Peter's inner ear. I barely let myself sleep on it. It seemed ridiculous to me that I would invite a dog to ruin something that I enjoyed explicitly for its immaculateness.

Peter slept in his crate the first night. The next day, while I was typing on my laptop in bed, he popped up on the side, lifting his body up by his paws, and surveyed the on-top-of-the-bed situation. He didn't jump up—oh, he wouldn't dare!—he was just politely checking it out. Seeing what was going on up there. He looked like a seal popping up from the water, with slicked-back ears, a little smooth head, gigantic eyes, and, well. God damnit.

Now we sleep together always. And unless it's a particularly good day, the best parts are always in the morning in bed with Peter and at night in bed with Peter. This is due to the soothing presence of his soft, warm dog body and the mollifying sound of breath traveling in and out of his tiny nostrils, but it's compounded by the fact that my favorite place on earth is bed. It is just the best place out there. It's soft and you get to sleep in it. It's at home, and I love being at home. As a thought exercise, I'd like you to try to imagine a single place on earth better than your own bed. Immediately I know what you're thinking—"the beach." Okay. I also like the beach. The sound of waves, et cetera. Lying down on a towel in the warm sun with your eyes closed. It's very nice. If each of us had our own personal beach inside of our homes I might say you had a point, but the fact is to own your own personal beach you have to have an immoral amount of wealth, and while of course we'd all like to have the ability to be immoral in that way, we likely won't be able to. In our lifetimes, it's hard to imagine any of us will be able to accumulate the amount of wealth it would take to have our own beach or even access to a shared private beach.

Instead, you have to go to a beach. You have to get all of your things together, get in the car. Try not to get sand in your wallet. Get sticky, then drive home with sand on your legs, and then there's sand on your bathmat. Is the beach really there for you in the way that your bed is? Quietly, humbly, and without expectation? Except for the dog hair, your bed doesn't really have any tactile debris that attaches itself uncomfortably to your body. Unless it's close to a window, your bed doesn't give you a sunburn. You're unlikely to be stung by a jellyfish in your bed, or drown. Or get bitten by a shark. Or see someone from work, and now you've both seen each other in what is essentially underwear. Your bed has pillows and blankets. Your bed has sleep. And if you're lucky, your bed has your dog.

When it's time for bed I'll ask Peter, "Do you want to go to bed?" He doesn't really have any agency in the situation, since he is technically my prisoner, but I like to offer him the illusion. He's always thrilled at the prospect and bounds away to my bedroom. That is, unless it's past 11:00 p.m.; generally if I haven't already gone to bed by 11:00, he'll put himself to sleep, trotting to my room in silence before jumping on the bed and plopping himself down, a man deciding what he wants to do and going about his business.

While in bed we'll usually sleep separately, with me the standard human way, and Peter either curled up at the foot of the bed or burrowed under the covers. One of my favorite interactions with him is when he noses me on the shoulder to let me know he'd like me to lift up the covers and allow him underneath. *You want to go under?* I ask every time, even though

I know the answer. (He does.) Once, my friend William was watching him for a few nights and told me that it took him a while, but he finally figured out why Peter kept shoving his little wet nose into his shoulder while he was trying to sleep. He was as excited as I was at the revelation—it was just interspecies communication to facilitate maximum comfort.

At some point in the night Peter tends to cuddle up to me, and I'll often wake up to find him with his little head on the pillow next to mine. At this point I'll either force-cuddle him or just watch his little sleeping face and listen to him breathe until the alarm goes off.

People can get a little squeamish about dog-human co-sleeping. This is wrong, so I thought it might be useful to enumerate the reasons why they get squeamish and then forcefully shut them down.

1. THEY THINK IT'S GROSS

Well, yeah, it is gross. Basically, in order to enjoy sleeping with your dog friend you just have to pretend it isn't disgusting. Convince yourself that you aren't affected by the fact that you have to lie in repose among the many things that have fallen off a dog's body. It's essentially a meditative practice. We're accepting it, and we're lying down, and we're moving on.

My bed is full of Peter hair at all times. It's sort of impossible to make it not be that way. I change my sheets and wash my duvet regularly but the amount of time it exists without dog hair is: never. The moment I put my sheets on the bed they are haired. It seems like the very air in my apartment is Peter hair, floating around, just waiting to settle on any available surface. It's fine. I had a friend in college who kept his mattress on the floor, and he would periodically "sweep the bed" if he thought he might soon entertain a woman, because the bed would attract dirt and other floor detritus. I thought this practice was revolting for several reasons but I now own a hand-broom with rubber bristles made specifically for "sweeping the bed" to remove dog hair, et cetera, and actually it's fine. It's fine.

And while we're here, I'm pretty sure most men under thirty don't even know they're supposed to ever change their sheets, and that's definitely grosser than this.

2. THEY THINK YOU'RE "SPOILING" THE DOG

In my opinion, eat shit. Excuse me; that was a little heated. I'll start again. In my opinion, eat shi—ah! Oh gosh. Okay. My apologies. In…my…opinion…—gah, oh no…eat… oh jeeze.

3. THERE IS A SOMEWHAT, WELL, LET'S FACE IT, SEXUAL CONNOTATION ASSOCIATED WITH SHARING A BED

The fact that I'm constantly telling Peter that he's the hand-somest man alive and that I want to marry him is bad optics,

I admit, but I do feel like this idea says more about the idea-haver than it does about me or you.

4. THEY THINK DOGS ARE DISRUPTIVE TO SLEEP AND HEALTH

This one will take longer to forcefully shut down.

I am not a good sleeper. I don't really have an idea of how it feels to sleep through the night, though I did once wake up from a surgery feeling remarkably well rested. I have dreams, I wake up, I toss and turn. Peter is similar. I've known dogs you could pick up and move from one location to another without interrupting their sleep, but Peter is sensitive. If you so much as move your eye in his direction—if you so much as *think* about him—he pops up. *YES?* his eyes say. *YOU WERE THINKING ABOUT ME?*

If there is a way he disrupts my sleep, it's that I'm always listening for anything that could possibly mean he's in danger. A hiccup, a cough, a particularly loud sigh, a murderer in the closet. I am nervous, alert, and ready to take action when necessary. Peter is, again, similar. He checks in if he hears me sniffling, he appears at my side if I take a breath too quickly, he's very alarmed if I sneeze. We spend much of the night worrying about each other.

It's possible that sleeping together is disruptive to both of us, but I think only in the way that buying scented candles is disrupting my ability to purchase a home. Yeah, it's probably not helping, but it's not like...the *main* issue. We are maybe not the most representative case. To get a sense of how sleeping with dogs affects the rest of humanity, I turned to the closest place I could think of to find a human: an internet forum. I found one called "Gun Dog Forum," which is a forum for those with gun dogs, which I found out are dogs trained to assist hunters. I am certainly not a hunter, nor is Peter a gun dog. It's the perfect place to deepen our pool of knowledge.

In a posting called "Where do your dogs sleep?" a forum member asks the community where their dogs sleep. She was originally against the idea of letting her nervous dog sleep in her bed, but was potentially persuaded. "Then, my roommate was like, 'just put him in bed with you,'" she wrote. "I retaliated with all of this nonsense about how it could create problems in the future, how I want to be the alpha, and such I read on the internet. And she asked me to explain the issues it could cause, and I didn't really have an answer." Huh. Well, what does the Gun Dog Forum—a forum that does, as you may have suspected, have a pinned "NO POLITICAL POSTS IN THE OFF-TOPIC CHANNEL" notice—say to that?

"I have three," responded a poster named Joe. "One sleeps in a crate and the other two sleep on dog beds. Absolutely no dog sleeps with me. I have a wife that eats up most of the bed, and I will not share anymore room with a dog. They are dogs not kids, not a wife. They need to know there [sic] place." A poster named Sharon quoted his cogent response.

"Exactly," she said, "well said." You can imagine her looking at the computer, nodding.

And indeed, it is true that dogs are not kids, nor are they a wife. And speaking of wives: "My wife moved into the other bedroom a few years ago due to 'our' snoring," said a user named Moomps, "so the dog and I share the bed now." A lovely arrangement, I think you'd agree. "My next house is going to have a Man room with tile floors," said the wistful Waterdogs1, "and a door going to a airing yard and it will be for dogs and me and dead animals on the wall." It sounds like paradise.

Those who responded were divided on the issue; some said their dogs slept in their own area of the house, others said they slept in their bed. And if they slept in their bed, it seemed to be either fine or annoying. An interesting bit of data. But what do my "friends" think, "friends" meaning a few friends but mostly the strangers who follow me on Twitter?

I constructed a form. "Do you sleep with your dog?," I asked. "How do you feel about your decision?" I received 101 responses, which reminds both of us of the movie *101 Dalmatians*. A little over 30 percent said they did not sleep with their dogs, for reasons like this: "It's annoying when he wakes me up." "Partner said no (allergies, sex)." "Sex with spouse prioritized over dog's codependency." "I'm a super light sleeper, plus I have white linens. These two factors, combined with the fact that I'm kind of a germaphobe = no dog on bed." A few said they'd like to sleep with their dog, but that their dog preferred to sleep elsewhere. One, who in fact does sleep with his dog, said, "My wife decided. I really hate it. We both sleep badly any night the dog is restless at all, and hygienically it's pretty disgusting." And of course I wish him the best of luck.

While there is some guilt in some of their situations (the sex-with-spouse one said he feels "reasonably good, occasionally guilty"), most of them said sleeping apart felt like the best decision for both them and their dogs. A bit less than 70 percent felt otherwise.

"She snores so I don't sleep as well as I used to before her but I don't care as long as she's happy," said a woman named Meghan. "It's nice when she's in the bed. But sometimes it's hot and sometimes she kicks us," said a guy named Matt. "She insisted; she's an Italian greyhound who wants to be under blankets and touching us always," said another guy named Paul. And how does Paul feel about it? "Not good!"

An overwhelming amount of responders said their dog had been the one to make the decision regarding their sleeping arrangement: "He decided for us." "I didn't decide, she decided." "He decided on his second night." Others never considered not doing it, and a few altered their behavior after life events. "My wife and I were strict adherents to crate training and a no-dog-in-bed policy. Then we had a miscarriage, and while my wife was recovering she brought the dog in the bed with her during the day, in his dog bed, because nothing is more therapeutic than cuddling with him. There was no going back."

For those who slept with a dog, even those who noted it made sleeping more difficult, the responses were almost unanimous: They felt great about it. "Wouldn't have it any other way. His dog snores help me sleep." "He's annoying to sleep with and hogs the bed, but I still get upset if he tries to sleep anywhere else." "Sometimes we feel like we are weak for sharing our sleeping space with a 75 lb beast who often sleeps like a starfish. People who are more disciplined dog owners often cast shameful looks while they judge us lesser owners for not having 'boundaries.' But I'll take waking up to a peaceful, loving, happy dog every day of the week."

Indeed, Neil. (That last guy's name was Neil.) Peter does not do the starfish move, but he does do several others that he seems to enjoy most when they are performed right in the center of the bed. Here is an abridged list:

√ **Cinnamon roll:** Curled, circular, ready to be picked up by a large spatula.

√ **Superman:** Arms stretched out before him, soaring through a dream.

√ **Gossip sphinx:** A modified "sphinx," which is when he sits like a sphinx, gossip sphinx finds his head lowered between his paws, perched and ready to hear who did what.

√ **Cow baby:** With arms and legs stiff and straight, oh he is just a little cow baby.

√ **Little man:** Smushed up right next to you, head on a pillow; the littlest man in town.

But my favorite is the "sleepy boy." Head smushed, peeking out from covers, resting on his paw. His eyes blinking slowly, fighting sleep like a child. A big sigh. A twitch of the nose. Boundaries are for suckers, Neil.

It seems to me the disruption in sleep is, if not nothing, at least negligible enough to most cosleeping dog owners that they don't feel a need to change their behavior because of it. But I suppose we should consult science.

Until recently, pretty much the only information we had about the effects of cosleeping with a dog was related to zoonotic diseases, which are diseases that can be transmitted from animals to humans. I asked Dr. Bradley Smith, of Central Queensland University in Australia, if I should be afraid of anything particularly zoonotic. "The transmission of zoonotic disease is so low it's ridiculous," he told me. "If your dog is healthy and vaccinated there is basically no risk." Okay—good.

Smith, a canine researcher who works at the university's sleep institute, noticed there was a dearth of studies that looked into the sleep-quality-related effects, either positive or negative, of cosleeping with a dog. The prevailing theory was that sleeping with dogs was disruptive to sleep, but the idea had been accepted without accompanying evidence, instead just judged by perception: that cosleepers are too often woken up by a dog's presence, or his shifting, or by the fact that you'd just like to look at his cute little face because he is sleeping so sweetly. "I have to say that there was basically no research on cosleeping with dogs," Smith said. "I found that weird, because about half of people, or households, own a dog, and about half of those co-sleep, either in the bed or bedroom."

Smith's research made use of actigraphy to study whether dogs disrupted their owners' sleep. Five female dog owners, and their dogs, wore activity monitors for seven nights, and then their activity over the course of the night was compared. I hate to tell you this, but the dogs did, in fact, negatively impact sleep. Dog movement typically led to human movement, and humans were 4.3 times more likely to be awake during dog activity than inactivity. "Co-sleeping with a dog appears to result in measurable, but relatively mild, reductions in overall sleep quality," the study concluded. "This detrimental impact must be weighed against the benefits of co-sleeping."

I asked Smith what this meant. Does science suggest I stop sleeping with my sweet dog whom I love so much, even though he has such sweet eyelashes, and I love to kiss his doggy face, and *even though* sleeping with him provides me with more joy than any other element of my life? Or what? "Can I be a real scientist and say 'it depends'?" he asked. Ugh. If you must. "I say this because there are just so many variables. For example, the number of humans and dogs in the household, the size of the dog, the size of the bed, whether the dog is toilet trained, the list goes on."

Basically he said that although the science indicates that, just like any cosleeping partner, dogs can cause sleep disruptions, the disturbances don't really cause a problem in terms of daily functioning. "That is," he said, "the impact is negligible." Plus, when asked to record their own experience, people report fewer disturbances than they experience. "I take this to be that the benefits of co-sleeping, for those that do it, far outweigh the negatives."

Well, well, well. It seems this reason is looking *pretty* forcefully shut down, after all. And can I tell you something else? *I hope it's not something about another study*, you're thinking, and, well, in fact it is. I'm sorry. This 2018 study, inspired by Bradley Smith's work and published by researchers at Canisius College in Buffalo, New York, surveyed 962 women living in the US. It found that 55 percent slept with a dog, 31 percent slept with a cat, and 57 percent slept with a human. And do you know what? The women with dogs, according to the study, were more likely to have a restful night.

"Compared with human bed partners, dogs who slept in the owner's bed were perceived to disturb sleep less and were associated with stronger feelings of comfort and security," the study says. It is true that whenever Peter hears a noise he looks toward its origin, which makes me feel very secure and protected from the radiator. The paper continues, "Conversely, cats who slept in their owner's bed were reported to be equally as disruptive as human partners, and were associated with weaker feelings of comfort and security than both human and dog bed partners." Ha-ha, of course, to cats.

In the end, my pink duvet cover got absolutely destroyed. Peter peed on it twice, vomited on it several times (most memorably after I'd mistakenly given him a rather large meat treat), and finally tore an enormous hole in it. It's fine. After the hole got too big I threw it away.

CHAPTER 7.5 HOW MUCH DOG HAIR DO WE HAVE IN OUR LUNGS?

The average adult breathes in about two thousand gallons of air every day. Since some of us spend our days and our nights in tiny living spaces that are wall-to-wall and floor-to-ceiling carpeted in dog hair, including the bathroom as well as, apparently, our bath towel, since there is hair on your body even after you get out of the shower, it might feel reasonable to ask—am I breathing in dog hair? And is it going to slowly fill up my lungs until I die?

"So the good news is—no," said David A. Hill, MD, chair of the Northeast Regional Board of the American Lung Association, assistant clinical professor of medicine at the Yale University School of Medicine, and owner of a Chihuahua–cattle dog mix named Snickers. Oh good!

"Our airway defenses"—cilia and mucus mainly—"are good enough to keep particles the size of dog hairs from getting in our lungs. The issue with dog hair in general is more dander related." Dogs and cats both lick themselves, then the saliva dries in their hair, and then it flakes off. "But if you're not allergic it's not an issue for you, other than you have to clean dog hair off of yourself and your apartment. For hair to get all the way to the lungs…it would have to bypass the defenses, and you'd have to really go out of your way to do that."

I asked if this was different for dog groomers, who have, presumably, smaller pieces of dog hair flying directly into their faces all day, and he said still no; they just have a higher risk of dander exposure. "But you actually made me go out and do some research," he said, which I hope is impressive to you, in case you were maybe thinking this question was stupid, even though I know your rudeness likely has nothing to do with me and you're just lashing out because I am your friend and you feel safe doing so. "There is a thing called 'dog groomer's lung,' but that has to do with…they use certain chemical sprays while they're grooming, or some of them do, and the chemicals in the sprays can cause a chronic allergic reaction. So it's not the hair." Damn. Or wait, sorry, I forgot what I was hoping for. Good!

So seems like we're fine, then. We just have dog hair in our showers, and in our beds, and on our pillows, and on our clothes, and on our face, and on our legs, and on the bottoms of our feet, and in our dinner, and in our candles, and under the tape anytime we use tape, and in our glass of water, and on our computer, and in our mouth. But not in our lungs!

Chapter 8

DOES MY DOG LIKE MUSIC?

Peter is not a very agreeable guy, in general. I really like that about him. It's not that he has a bad attitude—he's incredibly sweet, and if you say a bad word about him I'll harm you physically, ha-ha, "just kidding"—he's just not easily won over. He's not very doggy in that way, excited about anything and everything that might cross his path. He's not the type to go insane over just any new treat or toy. He's reserved. He takes his time to assess, and he's honest about how he feels. He knows what he likes: the kind of bacon treat that you have to keep in the fridge, his plushy platypus. And he knows what he doesn't: Ornette Coleman's *The Shape of Jazz to Come.*

The first time I put the album on in his presence, his head SHOT up from resting position—*what is this?!* An influential album in the free jazz style. *Okay, well...I'm not sure the atonality particularly suits my taste...* He was visibly annoyed, making direct eye contact while he shifted around, communicating his restlessness clearly, until I put on something more palatable to him. While I don't agree, I do understand. *The Shape of Jazz to Come* is not the easiest thing to listen to, and it in fact sounds nothing like the music dogs "like," if we're to believe the sort of music made for dogs is the sort of music dogs like.

That sort of music is like—well, have you heard it? You can find it if you search "DOG MUSIC" on YouTube or Spotify, or wherever. There are some outliers, some dog albums that are actually pretty good, but most of it is like if spa music were somehow less distinctive; it's what you would produce if you got a job providing live musical accompaniment for a yoga class without having any prior experience with music and only a vague idea of yoga; it's like if you programmed a Casio keyboard with "soothing" noises—birds, OOOOOOMMMMs, tones, chimes—and played them all at once.

That isn't to say it doesn't work. It is strange magic, dog music. Almost all of it, even the bad stuff, seems to calm Peter. He relaxes, he lies down on the couch, he goes to sleep. But I don't know that this means he *likes* it, necessarily, which seems to be the idea implied in "dog music"—music that dogs like. The sound of rain makes me sleepy, but that doesn't mean my favorite kind of music is "the sound of rain." Almost any podcast annoys me to slumber, but that definitely doesn't mean my favorite kind of music is "almost any podcast."

Instead, my favorite music is the band Spoon. And they don't make me sleepy at all!

I was more fanatical about music in my youth and, in fact, went to school to become a recording engineer. (Similar to a producer except more technical and less glamorous, though sometimes the jobs are done by the same person.) I only switched to English after I found recording engineering was too hard, and too much having to do with math. No thanks. I was not good at it. The class that weakened me was "microphone placement," ugh, but the class that broke me was "live sound." Absolutely impossible. And I had to take Music Theory III twice. Awful. I don't even want to think about it.

But because I enjoy music, I provide it for Peter, too. Almost constantly. Sometimes I play guitar for his pleasure, but mostly I just sing. I change the lyrics of popular songs to be about him; I sing about whatever activity he's doing. I had this cassette tape when I was little that featured songs with my name in them. (More in the custom-keychain sense than like Air's "Kelly Watch the Stars," one of the very few songs that has my name in it, which is a tip for songwriters who maybe need an underused name to put in one of their songs.) I remember the entirety of one of them and sing it for Peter, replacing my name with his. I think there would be copyright issues involved with telling you the lyrics exactly, so I'll just give you the gist: It was about how I was the greatest, amazing, stupendous, funny, smart, had a lot of heart, and was going to go far. Rather prescient, I think you'd agree. It rings just as true for Peter.

I also have a stable of short original songs that are good for anytime. I think the melodies are somewhat inherent to them, so I'll provide them here for your own singing pleasure:

- "Who is this little puppy man? He's doing everything a puppy can! He is little and he is sweet, and he has got— puppy feet!"
- "Who is this little puppy man? I love him all that a puppy can! He is little and he is funny and he has got—a puppy tummy!"
- "Are you my little puppy guy? Do you have little puppy eyes? Are you sweet and are you small? And do you have a face?"
- "Who is this little puppy guy, why is he so sweet? He is tiny and he is small, and he has got four feet!"
- "This is my best friend [kiss]. And I'll love him till the end [kiss]. He is little and sweet [kiss]. And he has got— puppy feet."
- "Why are you so small? (Chk-chk-chk.) And why are you so sweet? (Chk-chk-chk.) Why do you have a tail? Chicka-chicka, and why do you have feet? Chk-yeah!"
- "You are a munch and I love you a bunch, you are tiny and so soft to tou(n)ch! You are my baby and you're my man, I love you all that a puppy can!"

They're sort of derivative of each other, I suppose, but I think you'll agree that the song I sing for him while he's eating dinner is an exciting departure from form:

- "Munchman, munchman, munch-a-crunch! Muncha-muncha-munchaman, munch-a-crunch!"

Though it is clearly already quite good, I was curious if I might be able to improve my musical output. Peter deserves everything, including the ability to regularly hear music that pleases him, so if I can make it a little more like whatever that is I want to do it. So I reached out to Terry Woodford, one of the main guys who comes up when you Google "dog music."

Woodford didn't always make dog music. In the '60s and '70s he worked as a record producer, music publisher, recording engineer, and songwriter, and wrote songs for people like Jimmy Buffett, the Temptations, Alabama, and the Supremes. In the '80s, after being challenged by a day-care provider to make a record that could be used at naptime, he pivoted.

"When you hold a baby next to your chest, they can feel, if not hear, your heartbeat. So I thought, why not make that the drums." Up to the challenge, he recorded a human heartbeat and set simple arrangements of common lullabies to it. The music was tested in hospital nurseries and hospital staff said that it seemed to make babies stop crying. Then he got a call from a cardiac recovery unit in Alabama; they used his music to calm down babies after open-heart surgery, and invited him to come see. "It was pretty humbling and intimidating, and I had to put my head between my legs to keep from passing out." As Woodward tells it, he watched an infant's heart rate go down and breathing become regulated after the hospital staff turned on his music, and decided to leave the music industry to work on the baby music full-time.

"The dog thing, how that came about was I used to get calls from people who said that same CD that calmed their granddaughter worked to calm their dog." He says he didn't immediately buy it. "These are probably people who project human characteristics on their dog." People who do what, ha-ha?

He didn't know anything about dogs at that point and didn't have one (he has border collies now), but he was intrigued, so he sent the CD to a few kennels. "And I put a picture of a dog on it. I called it *Canine Lullabies*, and I said 'research done on human babies first.' I wasn't taking it too seriously." But it seemed to work for dogs, too—he got feedback saying it helped to stop barking, anxiety, and diarrhea. "However, there was one kennel in Connecticut that said they thought my music was pretty strange, and their dogs preferred smooth jazz. So, you know."

The music is pretty strange, for the record. Fluffy, syrupy vocals slowly singing nursery rhymes and lullabies over bare-bones twinkly music and an audible human heartbeat. It wouldn't feel out of place as the slightly, but only slightly, incongruous music played during the trailer for a horror movie about a murderous baby.

If you want, you can see the music working to calm down dogs in a Colorado Humane Society on the Canine Lullabies website. While a spectacularly creepy version of "London Bridge" plays over a stereo the dogs do, indeed, stop barking and lie down. "I didn't know the importance of it, I didn't realize it could make them more adoptable, and I didn't realize how anxious and upset they get from being there, being displayed, their routine being altered—like they're in prison, basically."

His music seems to calm Peter down, too, so I wanted to know if Woodford had any advice for me. I want to sing to Peter the best I can, like I said, and ideally I would like to write him a song. "All right, first of all," he said, "the lyrics don't mean anything." This is because dogs don't speak human language. Got it. "Maybe say the dog's name—they'll recognize that. They might recognize the names of their toys. What they will respond to is your voice, the compassion and caring in your voice if you're singing it." He said to keep it simple, keep it in tempo, and keep it predictable. "If you were to say something—I love you, let's say, and you're talking to your dog—the way you say 'I love you' to your dog is going to be different than the way you say it to a human." (It's actually not, but I get what he's saying.) "Whatever your melody is, make it follow the notes the way you'd speak it. That makes it more real. You're trying to sell a message and an emotion to your dog."

I liked this idea, but I wasn't sold on the lullaby aspect. It creeps me out, if I'm being honest. But I'm not super into the spa style, either. I wanted Peter's song to be something he would actually like. I remembered seeing a study aggregated on several blogs about how dogs preferred reggae over other styles. Maybe he would like reggae?

For that study, performed in 2017 by the University of Glasgow, dogs in a rehoming center were played soft rock, Motown, pop, reggae, and classical music, while researchers monitored their physiological and behavioral changes. They found that, in general, pretty much any sort of music worked to calm them down. They stopped barking, their heart rates lowered. While the dogs had their own individual preferences, the genres that had the highest success rates were soft rock and reggae. They "showed the highest positive changes in behavior," Professor Neil Evans said in a press release.

"The key, though, is variety," Evans told me. If a song was played over and over again, it was as if the dog just stopped hearing it; it stopped being effective. Plus, he noted, if you're choosing music to soothe your dog while you're away from home, and you play the same thing for your dog every time you leave the house, they're likely going to associate it with your leaving. "And that might cause more anxiety—'oh no, it's the going away song.'"

The results of my own experimentation with Peter were, honestly, a little surprising. He seemed to greatly prefer silence to "soft rock," and I feel the same. He likes Motown fine and seemed to be pretty into classical piano, but not orchestral pieces—they were too much, and I don't blame him for thinking so. He mainly likes Chopin. I played Spoon for him, a band he has heard many times before, and watched his response. He stayed...basically the same. It seems he tolerates Spoon fine.

For the record, I essentially judged this by whether or not he displayed sleepy behavior. While it does seem odd to me that this is how we decide whether a dog likes a certain type of music (rather than whether or not it...gets them hyped up, I guess), sleep does seem pretty integral to the dog experience. And you don't want them to feel unsettled. With Motown and Spoon he seemed calm, and with classical he eventually closed his eyes and fell asleep. But one genre led him to immediately stop what he was doing, jump up on the couch, and cuddle up into my legs for sleep, and that was, indeed: reggae. (Instrumental reggae in particular.)

So I guess his song should be reggae, or at least incorporate a steady reggae beat.

I know the song is for Peter, but as the songwriter I felt I needed some guidance from someone whose songwriting skill I admired. I don't think my art would ring true to Peter if it were not at least inspired in part by my own taste. "Have you ever written a song before?" Britt Daniel, of the band Spoon, asked. "No," I said. "Okay."

Britt is also one of my favorite vocalists, which, I think you'd agree, raises an interesting question. What famous male singer's voice would Peter's voice sound like if he could sing? It's something I've spent a considerable amount of time contemplating. We can discuss it together—I'll say what I think first, and then you write down what you think and save it for the next time you have a lull in conversation with a friend.

Freddie Mercury's voice is too powerful, obviously. Peter's charm is a harder sell than Sam Cooke's. David Bowie is closer, but ultimately too weird. Frank Sinatra's masculinity is too unexamined; Bruce Springsteen's masculinity is examined but still not right. Prince? Peter would be so flattered at the comparison, but no. Jello Biafra? Hm. I do think there are a lot of dogs out there whose singing voices would sound like Jello Biafra's, but not Peter.

I asked friends what they thought his singing voice might sound like and they said "Elliott Smith" and "Lou Reed singing 'Pale Blue Eyes.'" (You can see what sort of personality they think Peter has from their answers.) These are close, but I don't think they're quite right. Peter's voice would be at once rugged and angelic; capable of full-throated power but always maintaining a careful delicateness. An ethereal, lilting vibrato. Peter would sound like Jeff Buckley.

Britt: Have you ever sung melodies before, just for fun?
Kelly: Yeah, I have songs that I sing to my dog already.
Britt: Uh-huh.
Kelly: I just haven't tried to put them to, you know, actual music.

Britt: I see. So, these songs—do they have melodies?
Kelly: Sort of, yeah.
Britt: And do they have words?
Kelly: Yeah.
Britt: So you've pretty much got a song there.

Britt said (I'm calling him by his first name because I consider him a friend rather than a reportorial source) he doesn't generally write vocal melodies before he writes a song's music. "It's very rare that I write a vocal melody first. Not many of them are like that," he said. "'Metal Detektor' was like that." "Metal Detektor" is my favorite song of his, so in that case, I'm fine with having "written" the "vocal melody" first.

Britt: What are the lyrics about?
Kelly: His body parts mainly...that he's small and has ears
    and a face, and I love him.
Britt: Okay.

Britt was very encouraging about the fact that I'd already composed songs for Peter, though admittedly I did not disclose what the songs sounded like, nor did I give any examples of the lyrics. "Whenever I have lyrics and a melody I feel like I'm pretty much almost across the finish line. I think that's huge. Because often I write songs by coming up with melodies and chords, and then I gotta plug in lyrics, and that takes for-fucking-ever."

Personally I come up with my lyrics almost instantly, whenever I want to sing. I look at Peter, I see that he has a body and a face, I see that he has feet and is sweet, and inspiration strikes. "If you already have words about your dog that you feel are real, whether they're sentimental or funny or whatever they are, and you have these melodies, the first thing I would do is sing that melody, keep singing it, and find chords that work with it."

Putting my song lyrics to chords on the guitar was slightly challenging as I had maybe, in some instances, overstated how much of a "melody" I was working with. I was able to put some together, though. And emboldened by Britt's belief in my lyrics, I merged them into one super-song, sprinkled with Peter's name and the phrase "I love you."

Who is this little puppy man
He's doing everything a puppy can
He is little and he is sweet
and he has got
puppy feet.
Peter, Peter, Peter
Who is this little puppy man
I love him all that a puppy can
He is little and he is funny
and he has got
a puppy tummy!
I love you, Peter, Peter

Are you my little puppy guy
Do you have little puppy eyes
Are you sweet and are you small
And do you have a face
Peter, Peter, Peter
Who is this little puppy guy, why is he so sweet?
He is tiny and he is small
and he has got four feet!
I love you, Peter, Peter
This is my best friend
And I'll love him till the end
He is little and sweet
And he has got
puppy feet.
Why are you so small
And why are you so sweet
Why do you have a tail
And why do you have feet?
Peter, Peter, Peter
You are a munch and I love you a bunch
you are tiny and so soft to tou(n)ch
You are my baby and you're my man
I love you all that a puppy can!
I love you, Peter, Peter
Munchman
Munchman
munch-a-crunch!
Peter

The music is played on the upbeat, of course, with a human heartbeat sound I downloaded from the internet looped behind it. (Recording my own heartbeat proved too difficult. There are too many other sounds in the body; too difficult to isolate. I hope Peter isn't frightened by the dissimilarity, though I also had to alter the downloaded heartbeat significantly to fit the song's plodding rhythm, so I'm not sure he would recognize it even if I had been able to record my own.)

Does Peter like it? No, I don't think so. But one thing is for sure: It turns out that I *am* really smart at music.

CHAPTER 8.5: WHY DIDN'T BRUCE SPRINGSTEEN EVER WRITE A SONG ABOUT A DOG?

Doesn't it seem like Bruce Springsteen should have a song about a dog? Something like...a story about a guy who ditched his family, driving off in search of a more fulfilling life with only his dog by his side. Or like, maybe a song about how the dog is more free than the guy? Like a guy has a dog...and the guy will never know freedom, because he's stuck in a deadbeat town, but the dog is also stuck in the *same* town, and he's more free than anybody the guy has ever known. And it makes the guy think, like, is it the town that's the problem? Or is it the way I'm approaching living in the town? And then ultimately the guy concludes that...it's the town, yeah.

Something like that?

Bruce Springsteen lives on a farm in New Jersey with a bunch of animals, but the only recent evidence of his having a dog I could find is from a 2009 story in *New Jersey Monthly* written by a woman named Ingrid Steffensen. It's called "A Brush with the Boss" and recounts the time Steffensen and her dog, Arp, ran into Bruce Springsteen and his wife Patti Scialfa with their dog, Jackson, at the veterinarian's office. It's a lovely little meditation on fame. "To Arp, I am every bit as famous as Springsteen—and to Jackson, the Boss is just as ordinary as I am," she writes.

Jackson seems worthy of a song, to me. Springsteen also mentions a dog in his 2016 autobiography *Born to Run*. He says that in 1969, when he was living with his band in his family's old home on South Street in Freehold, New Jersey (the rest of his family had moved to California; I'm not gonna tell you his whole story, you can read the book yourself), a dog lived in the house, too. He describes him like this: "...a hell-raising, house-trashing, freely shitting mutt named Bingo."

Now, that basically sounds like a song already. So why isn't it? I attempted to track down Bruce Springsteen to ask him why he's never written a song about a dog even though I have evidence that he's known at least two, and, well, he is a difficult man to get in touch with, even if you have a really good question.

So I moved on to the next-best option: Bruce Springsteen tribute bands. I reached out to Tom Vitorino, the "Bruce Springsteen" in the Arizona-based Springsteen tribute band called the Rising and I asked him: Does Bruce Springsteen have any songs about dogs that I don't know about? And if not, why, when I happen to know for a fact that he's known at least two? "I don't know what Bruce's reasoning has been for his creative choices," Vitorino told me. Okay...

Vitorino said he thinks the line in Bruce's song "The Promised Land" (one of my favorites) is likely the most well-known mention of dogs in his catalog: "The dogs on Main Street howl, 'cause they understand, if I could take one moment into my hands." I would agree with that assessment. Vitorino also pointed out that while dogs don't seem to be a big part of his narrative, Bruce "seems to have really grown fond of horses over the last decade." His 2019 release *Western Stars* lean heavily into horse-and-cowboy-type imagery. "Leaving the inner-city characters of his early work, he continues to explore the universal themes of loss, love, and dreams, with a new backdrop for his characters."

—And yet no dogs?

Mark Salore, the Springsteen in New York–based tribute band called Tramps Like Us ("The #1 Bruce Springsteen Tribute Band," according to Tramps Like Us), told me he couldn't really recall a Springsteen song written about a dog. "There are a couple of mentions of a dog in various songs but nothing written about a dog," he said. "Hopefully this helps."

IT DOESN'T!!!!!!!!!!!!!!

Chris Cangeleri, the Springsteen in the also New York–based tribute band Badlands, is also a veterinarian. "Fun fact," he told me, "in addition to being lead singer for Badlands, I'm also a veterinarian." An incredible twist of fate, and indeed a fun fact. "There are only a couple of songs I can find where Bruce references dogs," he said. One is "Reason to Believe," which talks about seeing a man standing over a dead dog lying in a ditch. Not great.

The other one Cangeleri could recall was "The Wrestler," in which Bruce compares himself to a "one-legged dog." At least the dog isn't dead, but still not the feel-good dog anthem I was hoping for. "Pretty dark stuff," Chris said. Indeed. "Thanks" a lot. (Sarcastic.)

It seems I'm going to have to write my own Bruce Springsteen song about a dog, and that's just fine. I'm certainly up to the task. Please sing out loud to the tune of "Thunder Road."

The screen door slams, my dog's tail wags
Like a vision he rushes across the porch while I carry my bags
No I don't have any treats for you, boy
But I would like to give you some sweet joy
Okay, I bought some cheese, you just can have a little
  bit of cheese
Go run back inside, darling, and we'll go for a walk soon
So you're scared and you're thinking that maybe we won't go
  for a walk soon
Show a little faith! I promise that we will
But for now sit on your butt and just chill
Oh, while I put away . . . my things

You can hide 'neath the covers and lick on your paws
Seems if you had your druthers you would eat all your
  little claws
Chomping on your little tail
And licking around your penile sheath
Well now, I ain't judging, I understand
You have to clean your body and you don't have fingers
  or hands

But you're gonna make it clean, somehow
Hey, what else can we do now?
Except roll down the window, and not let your dog head
 out there!
I'm sorry, my buddy, but you just have to keep your
 head...in...here
I'm afraid you'll hit it on a pole
And that would really take a toll! (On my emotional and
 ultimately physical well-being!)
Climb in back, you're giving me a heart attack
Oh oh, give me your paw
We're riding out tonight, me and this little Chihuahua (mix)
Oh oh oh oh, Peter Road
Oh, Peter Road, oh, Peter Road
Lying out there like a sweetie in the sun
Hey, I know you're fast, you can make it if you run
Oh oh oh oh, Peter Road
Sit tight, take hold, Peter Road!

Well, I got this puppy and I wish I could make him talk
So he could say to me, "I am ready to take a long walk
"And, you know, I would like a treat"
Yeah right, buddy, all those treats ain't free!
But his words come across, even though unspoken
And okay he can have one, because my heart's broken!
You are my best friend, and I'll never let you go away!
I'll kiss you on your face, and I'll let you jump on me in
 the doorway

I'll parade you all around in the street
All the neighbors cooing at your sweet little feet!
And in the lonely cool before dawn
When you climb on me and yawn
I'll take you to the porch, you'll catch on, and then
    we'll go, yup
So Peter, leash up
It's a town full of losers—except for you my puuuuup!

Why did she pick such a long one? you're wondering, and
that was a mistake, yeah.

Chapter 9

CAN I TEACH MY DOG TO TALK?

Humans are the only species that can string words together with meaning. This seems a little unfair. Parrots are brilliant and can learn all sorts of sounds, and even which objects those sounds are attached to, but they can't tell us their parrot thoughts. Koko the gorilla could communicate words through sign language, but she lacked the capacity for syntax, and was never able to tell us if she thought Noam Chomsky was a dick. You can teach your dog to howl something like "AH RUH ROO," but does he really mean he ruhs roo? Or is he unwittingly participating in an emotional farce with the sole objective of potentially getting a cookie? Well. I don't want to be the one to spoil that for you, but I will suggest that you take some time to consider it.

Not being able to talk to your dog is, I think, one of the biggest mental adjustments you have to make after acquiring one. Or I guess I should speak in the first person in case you don't agree. Not being able to talk to my dog was one of the biggest mental adjustments *I* had to make after acquiring one (Peter). I bet you agree, though. It's weirder than having to handle bags of feces multiple times per day; weirder still than no longer feeling the need to participate in any social activities. Obviously dogs can't talk—I know "the rules," I'm not foolish. I understand that when they're shown to have a voice in film and television that voice is the voice of a human in I guess some sort of recording booth. I understand that when I do my "little boy dog voice" to say *"oh yes, yes, I wanna go outside, oh, MAMA!!"* that is me talking to myself. Still, it doesn't always feel right that he can't talk. It's a nagging feeling, one that was more intense right at the beginning of our relationship, but it hasn't fully subsided. The urge is, I think, similar to that of wanting to call someone who is no longer alive. You feel the pang and then remember. Oh. *Right.*

As for why, exactly, dogs can't talk, the animal behaviorist Mary Burch told me their brains "simply did not evolve so that they use speech." She works with the American Kennel Club and has allowed me to annoy her many times with questions similar to this one, due to my ostensible role as a member of the press. (This question was, for the record, "Why can't dogs talk?") "Further, the physical structure of the canine mouth is not well suited for talking," she said. "It is critical for humans to be able to place the tongue in a specific position, such as behind your front teeth to make the 'th' sound." Fine.

But it's hard to not feel about a dog the way you feel about anyone else. Any other human you're close with, I mean. Love, connection, and the urge to communicate are intertwined. The desire to know, the desire to understand, the desire to convince, the desire to ask if they want to watch a specific episode of *Sex and the City* or if we should just continue from where we left off last time. It feels natural, even if it also feels like something you shouldn't necessarily say out loud.

There's a modern-day wrinkle in this communication issue, too, that comes when you first realize, and truly come to terms with the idea, that you can't text your dog.

I don't imagine this feeling is entirely new. Probably in the past people felt bereft that their dog couldn't send them a letter tied to a pigeon's leg. Or maybe they thought, *I can't believe my dog doesn't know Morse code*. Or, *I can't believe my dog doesn't have a pager*. I think, though, this specific text-based pang of desire possibly says as much about our deep connection to our indispensable, desire-quenching phones as it does our need to communicate with our beloveds. *I'll just use my everything device to fulfill this nebulous emotional need.*

It's still bizarre, though. It seems like you should at least be able to let them know you're running late, or ask if they want anything from the store. Or like there should be a large doggy phone that you can send a text to, and the doggy phone (it would be chewable) makes a noise, and your dog can press it in response. Like, it has a large button. And then maybe the doggy phone device sends a text to your phone that says, "[YOUR DOG'S NAME] has pressed the phone." That would be a fine message, we don't need to pretend the dog is saying anything. It doesn't need to say "PUPPY LOVES YOU," or anything like that, we're all adults.

(If you make this you need to give me half of the money.) (Reading this is legally binding.)

When is she going to teach her dog to talk? you're probably wondering. *I thought this was going to be about how to teach your dog to talk, or, I mean, about how she taught her dog how to talk, or whatever.* Yeah, okay. I'll get to it. But first let me tell you about when I decided that I needed to teach him to talk. Settle in. Are you comfortable? Okay.

There wasn't a good dog park near the apartment I lived in when I first adopted Peter. There was one about a twenty-five-minute walk away, but it was a triangle situated between two busy streets, and that location made me nervous, even though I am generally extremely calm. Plus it was shitty. A hard dirt ground with rocks, no dog water fountain, generally some broken glass. You had to walk along a busy street to get there, and sometimes it can feel like dogs are just desperate to die in traffic. They pull on their leashes right toward the speeding cars—why do they do this? Do they want to chase the cars? Well. Either Peter wanted to chase the cars or he'd rather die than go to the shitty park, and I wouldn't allow either, so. We didn't visit that park much.

There was, however, a nearby secret off-leash area. This is a nice thing about living in the city—you sometimes have the ability to quietly conspire with like-minded neighbors about the righteous ways you're going to subvert laws, in this case for the purpose of giving your dog a slightly better life and thus relieving a small amount of the enormous guilt you feel for making them live in the city in the first place. This area was in a cute little park, grassy and shaded with trees, situated in a quiet part of the neighborhood. The park smells wonderful in the spring; it's green and leafy in the summer. In the winter it's more wintery. It's adorable.

Now, around the perimeter of this park was a wrought-iron fence. There was about eight feet between the park's fence and the high wooden fences that acted as a border between the neighboring properties. Though dogs were not allowed off-leash inside the park, I noticed, slowly, that owners were letting their dogs run in this otherwise unused space along the length of the perimeter, between the two fences. A bold and rebellious act—and quite seductive.

(This is where I'll bring up a minor issue. There were also dog owners who allowed their dogs to go off-leash in the main area of the park. I don't want to seem like a prude, but the park opens onto the street and there was ample possibility for dogs to escape and die. Plus having an off-leash dog attempt to play with an on-leash dog is not ideal, and was most often treated by the off-leash dog's human as, like, *oh, isn't this fun?*, and the answer was no, not really. Not for us. We're on a leash. We are restrained where some run free. We do not appreciate this, as anyone wouldn't. And it bothered the non-dog-owning park humans, thus drawing attention to the rest of us quietly breaking the other rule. This annoyed me, not that I'm not cool—I am very cool and actually everyone thinks so.)

But I digress. I'd see noninvasive dog parents in the secret off-leash section on my walks with Peter. In there, playing with a tennis ball, looking happy and free. *How did they get in there?* I wondered, as the fence didn't have a clearly visible gate. *Did they get down on all fours and train their dog to hop on their backs, and then over the gate? Or do they tunnel underneath? Were they born inside of the gate? Will they die in there?* It was a mystery—until one summer morning.

"How did you get in there?" I asked a woman who was in there with her dog.

"It opens over here," she said, pointing to the part where the gate opened.

Oh my god. I was stunned. That woman's answer did no less than completely change our life. For the rest of the summer, and fall, and winter, Peter and I would head to the park in the morning and afternoon and he'd excitedly drag me over to the exact part of the gate that opened, unable to contain his joy at the possibility—so close he could taste it!—of playing his favorite game, which is the game "chase," which is a game where I pretend to "try" and "catch" him while I say *I'm gonna getcha!* and he runs and runs and runs. It was blissful in the warm air, as it was in the crunchy leaves, as it was in the fresh snow.

We'd run into other dog owners at our secret spot, of course, and there were always rumors about the pigs. I talked to a guy, probably in his forties, with a dog a bit bigger than Peter. "They can give me a ticket if they want," he said, "but I'm not going to stop bringing him here." He'd been ticketed in the past but said it was worth it, cursing the city for not building our neighborhood the real dog park they'd promised years before. I immediately adopted his rebellious attitude. Give me a ticket, I dare you! We'll go on the lam—we have nothing to lose!

One late-winter day Peter and I took our usual walk to the park. He pulled me toward the gate, unable to contain his joy, as usual. When he reached the opening he sat while he waited for me to let him in, to allow him to experience happiness, to embark on his favorite part of the day. He has the sweetest expectant behavior when he's waiting for me to open a door. He just looks right ahead at his eye level. Generally a human would look at the knob, I guess, because they were going to use the knob. There's no reason why he would look up at the knob, or whatever other kind of opening mechanism the door has; obviously he doesn't know what that is or how it works, but looking at and expecting the door to open from its bottom third is just so sweet. *Why isn't the thing doing it yet?* I imagine him thinking, as he waits. *I can't wait for this thing to do what it does.*

As he was looking intently at the bottom third of the gate, sitting like a good boy, tail wagging, eager and full of expectation, I spotted it. A padlock.

I futzed with it for a moment before the horror sank in. Peter looked away from the gate and into my eyes. *Why isn't the thing doing it?*

I looked for other ways to get in. Could I somehow...get down on all fours and train him to jump onto my back and then over the fence? No. Was there a wide enough gap anywhere, that maybe we could fit into? No, of course not. I dragged him away, apologizing, explaining the situation out loud in human words. "The gate is locked, buddy, I'm sorry. I'm sorry, I'm sorry."

The gate stayed locked until we moved, and I desperately wanted to tell him why we stopped going. It wasn't his fault. It was the padlock. It was the pigs, or at least the Parks Department. They got us, after all.

That's when I decided that I needed to teach him how to talk.

There have been a few talking dogs. Sort of. In history, I mean. There was Don the Talking Dog, a large brown hunting dog who traveled from Germany to New York City in 1912 and made a name for himself in the US vaudeville scene. Don reportedly knew how to speak eight words in German; roughly the equivalent of how many words I know how to speak in German after having lived on the Stuttgart US military base for a few years as a child, taking German in high school for two years, taking German in college for four years, and taking a three-month post-college course in Manhattan of which I must admit I skipped several classes even though I elected to take it for no reason other than my own supposed desire and it cost $300.

The words Don knew, according to most sources, were "Don" (his name), "haben" (to have), "kuchen" (cake), "hunger" (hunger), "ja" and "nein" (yes, no), "ruhe" (quiet), and "Haberland" (the surname of his owner Martha Haberland). "Ich habe hunger" is a phrase I remember, if you're curious. I could also do something like: "Ja, ich habe hunger."

Don was a huge celebrity, captivating audiences across the country with his supposed ability to speak, at one point even sharing a bill with Harry Houdini. His act consisted of answering questions posed to him by vaudeville performer Loney Haskell, who would then interpret his German responses for the mostly English-speaking audiences. While on tour in San Francisco, Don met with J. C. Merriam, a paleontologist at the University of California at Berkeley, who according to accounts from the time "declared his belief that the dog can reason and think for himself."

Very interesting.

But not everyone was convinced. The journal *Science* reported in May 1912 that Don's speech was "to be regarded properly as the production of sounds which produce illusions in the hearer." A reviewer from the magazine *Variety* agreed, noting that the dog never asked questions, merely answered them, and concluding that "the trained growls which emanate from his throat can readily be mistaken for words." The writer also noted, though, that while the audience was skeptical, "after the first try they became interested and later enthusiastic."

Chaser the border collie knew 1,022 nouns, which is obviously pretty good. She couldn't say them out loud, but she could identify them by their corresponding objects. Her owner, John W. Pilley, a professor emeritus of psychology at Wofford College, worked with her for four or five hours every day to achieve this, telling her a word and showing her an object over and over, and then hiding it and asking her to find it; this object collection added up to eight hundred cloth animal toys, 116 balls, twenty-six Frisbees, and a collection of other plastic items. Chaser was known as "the smartest dog in the world" and could even determine the meaning of full sentences. Pilley died in 2018; Chaser followed him soon after in 2019.

More recently, a speech pathologist in San Diego, California, named Christina Hunger made headlines with her dog named Stella, who seemingly communicates her thoughts and desires through use of a soundboard. "This Dog Learned to 'Speak' and Says Exactly What You'd Expect a Dog to Say," the *Huffington Post* said. "Dog Learning to Talk by Using a Custom Soundboard to Speak: 'I'm in Constant Amazement,'" *People* said.

The videos of Stella "talking" through the soundboard are wildly popular on Instagram. No, wait, please don't leave to look at them, I'll explain them to you. In one, Stella—a beautiful Catahoula and blue heeler mix—presses a series of buttons: HAPPY, BALL, WANT, OUTSIDE. "Happy, ball, want, outside? Okay, we can go outside and play with your ball," Christina says. She explains in the Instagram caption that Stella was communicating her desire to go outside and play with her ball. This is convincing enough. It seems entirely possible that a dog could learn which button goes with which word—ball, outside—like Chaser with her toys. Other videos are less convincing.

"Jake and I were discussing taking Stella to Petco. She was certainly listening…!" Hunger wrote in a caption accompanying a series of videos, the first of which shows Stella pressing GOODBYE and OUTSIDE. (Because she wanted to "goodbye outside" to Petco, allegedly.) The next video shows Stella pressing LATER and JAKE, the button for Christina's partner, Jake. "Jake said he wanted to hang our spice racks first, started the project," Christina explained, "and Stella told him, 'Later Jake.'" She translated for us: "(Translation: Do that later, I want to go!)."

I'm not entirely sure if I believe a dog has the cognitive ability to tell Jake to hang the spice racks later because she wants to go to Petco now. But it would certainly help my theory that I will one day be able to teach Peter how to hold full conversations.

I have a friend named Brian whose pug Dita can say "ah ruuu roo." He says to her, "AH LOOFFF YOOOUU" and she says to him "AH RUUUU ROOOO!" It's very sweet. She also knows the names of several of her toys and can "throw away" trash, if the trash is a wad of paper that is placed in her mouth. (She can also un-throw-away trash, taking trash out of the trash can and scattering it all over the floor, effectively "teaching" Brian to "throw away" trash, which is what he deserves.) She is brilliant and I'm proud to know her.

There are lots of videos of dogs who can say "I love you" on YouTube—a lot of huskies, they're a very vocal breed—and lots of video tutorials so that you might teach your own dog how to do it, too. The way you begin is by teaching your dog the "speak" command. The way you do that is this: Do something you know is going to elicit a bark, attempt to say "SPEAK!" before the bark happens, and then immediately reward with a treat. I thought this would be a good place to start on the road to teaching Peter how to talk.

An immediate issue that we encountered is that Peter does not bark.

This is not to say he's never barked. Sometimes when he gets too flustered about an unreachable squirrel outside the patio door at my parents' house he will—as if he was desperately trying to hold it in, but had no choice except to ultimately succumb to its far greater strength—do one bark. And he once barked at a child. It's not his fault. He's generally great with children, I promise; he's put up with all manner of pets and awkward cuddling. But this time was different.

On this winter morning the city was preparing for snow. Peter was recovering from an injury that caused him to limp. As we walked out of our building and down the street, my back facing the direction of oncoming traffic, a salt truck, curiously silent, drove by and began furiously pelting us—a human and a canine who were ON THE SIDEWALK!—with ROCK SALT! I tried to shield Peter's poor little body, but he was pelted just like I was. We turned the corner. Halfway down the next street, again our backs to oncoming traffic, another CURIOUSLY SILENT SALT TRUCK drove by and PELTED US WITH SALT AGAIN! I couldn't believe it. This time I yelled "FUCK YOU!" at the truck while again trying and failing to shield Peter, which I know was wrong. Heinous, just heinous behavior on the part of both trucks, and then me. But I don't believe 8:00 a.m. is the correct time to attack sidewalks with a cannonade of rock salt.

And this was on top of the fact that he was already injured. As we entered our building a little boy approached Peter. "Can I pet him?" I said yes, incorrectly. After the boy touched Peter's head he unleashed his signature single bark, of course immediately making the boy burst into tears. "I'm so sorry, he's hurt, he didn't mean it, I think he's just a little scared, I'm sorry, he's not usually like this!" I apologized profusely to him and his dad, who was standing next to him. "See? He's hurt," the, luckily, very kind dad said. "You know how you don't feel good when you're hurt? He doesn't feel good. That's all."

The boy was not soothed.

So I guess in order to get Peter to bark and learn the speech command I could have injured him, pelted him with salt, and forced him to interact with a child. But I'm not particularly close with many children.

There is another option, though. Apparently a myth exists, mostly in Europe, that animals are able to talk on Christmas Eve. Not just dogs and cats—the myth goes for farm animals, too, and even bees. It pops up with different outcomes in a bunch of stories: In *The Christmas Troll and Other Yuletide Stories,* by Clement A. Miles, the animals gain speech and conspire against their uncaring owners; in a cartoon that aired on ABC in 1970 called "The Night the Animals Talked" the animals gained speech and were mean to each other, and then lost their ability to speak in a lesson meant to communicate that...people don't...spread the word of God enough? Or something. An English legend says that on Christmas Eve all the bees gather to sing a hymn, which I think you'd agree sounds very nice.

The reason for the talking is kind of fuzzy, but it seems to be based on the belief that the baby Jesus was born at exactly midnight and all the animals briefly gained speech at that exact moment in order to praise him. I assume they do it year after year just sort of out of habit. After failing to teach Peter how to talk, I thought I needed to at least try to see if he'd talk on his own for Jesus's birthday.

Just before midnight on Christmas Eve, Peter and I were together in bed at my parents' house. Not in my childhood room; my childhood room was cruelly given to my younger brother Thomas after I went away to college. Do I think now that we're both adults who live outside of the house that that room should revert back to its original owner? Of course. However, it is not up to me. The room I stay in is a guest room that used to be the office where I went on AOL for the very first time.

So we were in bed in the room just before midnight, in the dark. Peter was burrowed under the covers. As midnight approached I got underneath, too, and propped my head on my hands. I was ready to listen. I looked him in the eyes. I said, "Okay, Peter." The time turned to midnight. "Peter," I said, "Go ahead." I spent a lot of time attempting to use a Ouija board in that house, so the feeling was not wholly unfamiliar. "Peter. I'm listening." He looked me in the eyes and sat up. Oh my god. Was the moment coming?

He then stood up on all four legs. To say what? To tell me what news?

He turned around and resumed his curled position, now with his back to me, tired of whatever stupid bullshit I was doing so late at night. "Enough," he seemed to say. "Enough of you and your stupid bullshit."

Ah. It seems dogs do talk to us, after all.

ADDENDUM: DOGS SHOULD BE ABLE TO TALK FOR TWENTY-FIVE MINUTES PER DAY

I've actually thought of a pretty good solution to the problem of dogs not being able to talk. They should be able to talk but *just* for twenty-five minutes per day. I think that's a fair compromise. It's not a lot to ask, as you can see. It's just twenty-five minutes (per day). Of course I assume you have some questions.

If dogs can talk for twenty-five minutes per day, will they be aware of the fact that they can only talk for twenty-five minutes per day and feel trapped inside of their own minds until they're finally allowed to briefly speak?

No. Luckily, what I'm proposing is that everything would be normal for them the rest of the time. They would just be a dog and then they would speak.

Would they have a dog brain during the speaking time, or would they have more of a human brain? And what language would they speak?

Two good questions. They would have sort of a combo dog-human brain, so they were able to communicate with you while maintaining a certain dog-ness, and they would speak whatever language their owner speaks. Really, it would be more like the owner could finally hear the dog for twenty-five minutes per day, though the dog would, yes, also be imbued with a bit of human-like cognizance to make this form of communication (talking) easier.

When would they speak?

Well, this might cause a few issues. Normally it would be toward the end of the day, but really it wouldn't have a schedule and you certainly wouldn't be able to plan for it. If you're out during the speaking time—maybe you're at work, or in the shower—you're sort of fucked. And you won't even know it for sure until the day is over, when you would sit back and think, *Well. I guess I missed it.* That would be "ruff," ha-ha, especially if you needed to talk about something important.

But if you were around for speaking time, your dog would be able to tell you how he is, and you would be able to tell him about your day (he won't care) and ask him questions, like:

√ "Are you feeling okay?"
√ "Are you sad?"
√ "Am I making your life worse than it would be if you had another person taking care of you, maybe because I'm not fun enough or you just don't like me?"
√ "Do you think I'm a failure?"

√ "Do you know how old I am?"
√ "What if I tell you my age? Then you tell me if you think I'm a failure."
√ "Did you hear that loud bird this morning?"

Et cetera. Dogs could tell on their owners if they were mistreating them, too; maybe catch the ear of a friend or neighbor.

In that case, could they tell on their owners if they saw that they were doing something like cheating on their wives?

No. But maybe you should be afraid of that anyway, because who knows...maybe they could.

Would you be able to explain commands to your dog that you would otherwise have to teach him through normal dog training methods?

No. Dogs won't remember what goes on during the speaking times; you're not establishing a history this way. It's just a check-in. You'll need to teach your dog "sit" the normal way. However, when you do speak with him, you can compliment him on his sitting.

What if your dog doesn't like you and he's mean to you during his twenty-five minutes?

I wouldn't worry about that too much. I bet he likes you fine. And if he doesn't, maybe he can tell you what you're doing wrong that's making him hate you and you can fix that about yourself. Maybe you're annoying. Maybe you're selfish. It could be very good for you to hear things like this from a dog and then adjust.

If you tell him "I love you" during the talking period, will he understand what you mean?

Yes, and over time he will remember the feeling he gets when you tell him, so when you say it throughout the day he will also understand. This may seem like it doesn't align with the rule that you can't teach dogs things during the speaking time because they can't remember, but actually it has nothing to do with that. Okay?

So, that's the proposal. If you can, please get it into the hands of the government or Alexandra Horowitz or whoever is in charge.

CHAPTER 9.5: IF YOU SAY "I LOVE YOU" TO YOUR DOG EVERY TIME YOU GIVE THEM A TREAT, WILL THEY KNOW "I LOVE YOU" MEANS SOMETHING GOOD EVEN WITHOUT THE TREAT?

Okay, so my idea is that saying the words "I love you" at the same time I give Peter a treat (which is something that he likes) will make him feel a jolt of positivity that will carry over even when the treat element is taken away. Genius, yes? I reached out to Dr. Laurie Santos, the director at Yale's Canine Cognition Center. She had a pretty succinct answer:

Dogs are keen associative learners, meaning that anything associated over time (e.g., a sound and a reward) will come to be connected in a dog's mind. That said, once you get rid of the reward, you do break the association. So a better way to think about this is that a dog will come to expect that the sound "I love you" equals food.

Well. God damnit!

Chapter 10

CAN I COMMUNICATE WITH MY DOG VIA A PET PSYCHIC?

What do you think the color of Peter's favorite treat is? I'll give you one minute to guess, and then I'll tell you the alleged answer. This is a test of both our friendship and your integrity. Please don't let me down and stay within the allotted time (one minute). Okay, you can start coming up with your guess now.

It's brown! (Allegedly.) Or, to phrase it in the form in which it was revealed to me, "Does he have a brown treat?" The man who told me this, a pet psychic whom I spoke with for thirty minutes over the phone for $75, had telepathically asked Peter what his favorite treat was so I could give him more of that specific treat when he (Peter) was being a good boy. He's always being a good boy, so you can see how this information might be useful.

As you now know, Peter told the pet psychic, telepathically, that his favorite treat is brown. Incredible. What's more incredible is that Peter does, in fact, have a brown-colored treat. And what's more incredible than that is that he has several brown-colored treats. And what's even more incredible than that is that just about every dog treat I have ever seen in my entire life has been brown. Store-bought, homemade, peanut butter on a spoon—that's the color they all are: brown. (Okay, yes—the exception is Greenies. But the name of Greenies, I think you'd agree, clearly makes a point of disclosing that the treats are not the sort of color you might expect from a treat, which is: brown.) So . . .

The psychic was right!

"Pet psychic" is wrong, though—I want to clear that up immediately because after speaking with a number of pet psychics and liking many of them very much, writing "pet psychic" makes me feel guilty. The industry-preferred term is "animal communicator." I hope they can sense that my energy is apologetic. "Animal communicator" is favored for a number of reasons, including a general dislike of the implication that animals are subordinate and something one can own, and for its emphasis on the fact that the communicator is facilitating a two-way conversation rather than a one-way reading. They're not predicting the dog's future; the communicator instead invites the animal into a discussion. "Animal communicator" sounds slightly less silly than "pet psychic," too, which I imagine is a benefit.

Have you ever visited a human psychic? I haven't, but I once had a tarot card reading. It was a lot of fun, in large part because I did it as part of my job, so it was free, and otherwise it would have been $80. It was mostly a lot of compliments: The tarot reader said that I was a strong and powerful woman, that I was working on something that would change my life forever, that the only thing standing in my way was my own self-doubt, and that I had a strong presence in my life that supported me emotionally and inspired me creatively. At the time I was curious about why that last one didn't seem to resonate, as the rest of the compliments seemed, clearly, dead-on. In thinking about it since, I guess it's because I was trying to pin the description on a human. Maybe the cards were, instead, sensing Peter. That feels more correct; our first mystical connection.

I guess all the compliments were true, then.

It's obvious why someone might be tempted to turn to a communicator in order to talk to their beloved animal, even if that person is otherwise reasonable. It's terribly hard to share a life with a close friend with whom you are unable to speak. It would be nice to find out, at least, a few basic things. Are they okay? Are they happy? Do they like you? Would they have rather had the green giraffe toy with a squeaky butt, or are they okay with the purple elephant toy with the squeaky trunk? Do they feel safe? Do they know how much you love them? Are they happy? Are they happy? Please, god, just tell me this—*are they happy?*

What a communicator does extends beyond the novelty of finding out your animal's likes (brown treats, apparently) and dislikes (when your boyfriend is near you) and into heavier subjects, like the sources of behavioral abnormalities and illness. Some also offer the service of finding lost pets, but that is a bit more specialized. People will call a communicator to find out why their horse keeps bucking, or why their cat won't pee in her litter box. They'll schedule a session to find out if their dog is in pain. They'll reserve some time if their animal is dying and they just need help letting go.

And they pay. A half-hour phone session is generally around $75, but it can be double that, or more. A half-hour session from a communicator in Michigan who goes by "Lorrie the Pet Psychic" is $105; a full hour is $210. Laura Stinchfield, a communicator in California, charges $150 for a half hour, $275 for a full hour, and $550 for two hours. Emergency sessions are offered at a higher cost. In Stinchfield's case they begin at $200 for a half hour. Most sessions are conducted via phone because communicators can reach more clients that way, and because, as communicators will eagerly tell you, energy can be read over the phone just as well as it can be read in person.

But can an animal communicator really open up a path of understanding between a woman and the sweet dog whom she loves so much that it makes her want to die every single day of her life and like her internal organs are combusting one by one beginning with her heart? And, if so, how?

"Animal communication is very simply a process of becoming more aware of the images in your mind, the thoughts in your mind, and the feelings in your body," Diana DelMonte, an animal communicator in Los Angeles, told me over the phone. At the time we spoke she'd been a professional communicator for nineteen years. In conversation she's warm and charming, and when she talks about her work—which can be seen in many videos online, if you'd like to watch for yourself—she is incredibly convincing.

In one video titled "Animals Are Psychic. The Good News Is...So Are We!" she sits cross-legged in a chair at what seems to be some sort of holistic bookstore. She is calm and lithe with long gray hair tied loosely at her neck, a billowing white blouse, and a floor-length forest-green skirt; in other words, she looks exactly like what you would expect. She has a resonant, patient voice. In *Animals Are Psychic. The Good News Is...So Are We!* the movie, she would be played by Meryl Streep.

DelMonte specializes in communicating with animals who have behavioral issues, animals experiencing an illness, lost animals, and animals at the end of their life. The goal of a typical session is communicating to you how your animal is feeling; she does this by connecting to them telepathically and receiving the images they're sending, then passing them on to you to place them in context. In healing sessions she does a body scan of the animal to find where there might be physical pain, and a chakra diagnosis to find where there might be an emotional root to the pain. In testimonials on her website, customers praise her for being able to help her animals when their vet couldn't.

"Thanks to you Chewy is alive," says Lila Henry from Boise, Idaho. "The Vet had said he was in pain and gave him morphine! Chewy did not improve. He did not eat for two days. I told the Vet that you said it was his stomach, and that Chewy felt extremely nauseous. They gave him fluids, did a blood test and gave him anti-nausea medication. He went home and ate and drank. They never found out what was wrong with him, but he is getting better every day. You saved his life!"

And of course we're glad for Chewy.

DelMonte is one of a few animal communicators I spoke with for the purpose of what you are reading right now, as well as for my general life's purpose of one day being able to ask Peter if he likes my outfit or thinks I should wear something else. I'd imagined these conversations would feature me lightly dancing around the question of exactly how they...*do it*?—meaning, how they talk to animals telepathically and over the phone—until potentially gathering the courage to ask something similar to that question in veiled terms. This delicate touch was not necessary. Everyone was very okay with telling me exactly how they...*do it*.

Some of them even teach classes on exactly how they do it, and it was in those sorts of classes where many of them learned exactly how they do it in the first place. DelMonte teaches regular animal communication workshops in LA, but they're also offered by other communicators everywhere, in abundance, all over the country as well as online. Telepathic communication is not some great secret, or a gift for the few. It is, as everyone would tell me at some point in our conversation and usually right at the beginning, the most natural way any of us can connect with each other.

"Kids do it naturally. Mothers with infants, mothers with toddlers," Cathy Malkin, an animal communicator from Pleasant Hill, California, told me, regarding nonverbal intuition-based communication. (She, too, teaches classes, and learned communication under communicator Penelope Smith.) "Before we learn verbal language we're all doing it, we're born doing it. But then we value language, and if it can't be seen, it can't be measured. We don't value intuition.

"You're doing it on some level with Peter already," she continued. "Some of the basics. But what blocks us is that we invalidate ourselves. We have projections, our own thoughts and feelings can block our intuition, and sometimes we anthropomorphize animals...so it's not an authentic dialogue. But communication is a heart-to-heart connection, and the head does the interpretation."

(Cathy Malkin, I want to point out, has an excellent website. In one section about what you should expect from a session, various little images of animals are coupled with quotes about why you should give Cathy a call. It's very good. A parrot says, "Now my people know how to help me."

A horse says, "I love working with Cathy because everyone wins." A donkey says, "Best of all I don't have to leave my home to talk with Cathy." And that donkey is right—not having to leave your home is truly is one of the best parts of any home-based activity.)

It's true, of course, that Peter and I communicate somewhat intuitively already. Dogs communicate through body language—baring their teeth, wagging their tail, panting, looking into your eyes with an intensity that can only mean "PLEASE. I NEED TO PEE!!!!!!!!!!!!!"—and respond to subtle human cues in a way that can make it seem like they're reading your mind. Peter, for example, will run to his crate, his poor little tail fluttering in fear, whenever I even begin to walk toward the direction of where his toothbrush is kept. I try to tell him through subtle pained facial expressions: *My sweet friend, I am just trying to brush your teeth. I assure you this is for your benefit, and that your dog toothpaste is chicken-flavored, which the box assures me is pleasant for you. Please, just let me brush your teeth so your vet doesn't think I am bad.*

Animal communicators insist, though, that this connection goes beyond the reading of bodily cues. "A lot of times people will know something about their pet and they won't even realize they know it," Anne Angelo Webb, an animal communicator from New Jersey, told me. "For instance, someone's dog might be telling them that they have to go to the bathroom, and the person's just sitting there, walking around, whatever, and then all of the sudden they think—

I need to take my dog out, he's gotta go out. They overlook things like that."

Okay. So, if we can all do it...how do we do it?

"Some teachers will say you imagine a golden spiral going from your heart to your animal's heart," DelMonte told me. "Those methods are good to start off with, but really in essence you don't need to do any of that. You just have to think about your animal." Okay, amazing, I am already always doing that. Next? "You want to get out of your head. So you drop down to your heart center, and you set your attention on your heart center. So I just imagine being connected at my heart center with the animal, number one. Number two—"

Wait, I'm not ready for number two. I do not know what dropping down to my heart center means, but it sounds like "singing from your diaphragm," which is something I also do not understand. In discussion with these communicators and through additional research of my own, it seems the way you move out of the thinking mind and drop into your heart center is: by doing it. You shift your focus from your head to the physical center of your heart, you attempt to feel grounded there, and you take a few deep breaths, and that's it. Okay. We've done it. Now we can rejoin DelMonte.

"Number two: I see the animal's face in my mind's eye, and mentally I may call his or her name a few times. And that's it. You'll feel an exhilaration in your heart center when you're really connected. Then you just start asking your questions mentally, and you have to trust what you receive."

After learning this, I try to do it with Peter. I concentrated on the middle of my torso. I took a few deep breaths. I tried to clear my mind and waited to receive what he might be sending. *Shoes* popped into my head. *Pork chop.* Hm. These have no connection to Peter, so either I was communicating with a ghost, or (scarier still) my brain, once cleared of its usual chatter, was hardwired to fall back on fairly old-timey dog tropes. *Shoes* I kept being sent. *Pork chop.* Ugh.

Learning to trust what you receive when connected to an animal is the primary goal of animal communication workshops. Participants will often be instructed to bring photos of their own pets, in order to pass them to each other and see if they can affirm what their fellow classmates are receiving from the photographed animal's energy. You can imagine it now—a bunch of people sitting around, holding pictures of each other's cats. "I'm sensing um...that she...is agitated about another cat, somewhere?...And she...um, can make a pretty convincing argument that *Click* is Adam Sandler's best movie?" It's a fun activity you can force your friends to do at a party they'll immediately wish they'd thought twice about attending.

Here is something else I'm curious about, though, not that we have to dwell on it for very long. How the fuck—excuse me. How do communicators find lost pets? Or at least, how do they go about searching for them?

For some insight into this I reached out to Tim Link, a communicator from Georgia who specializes in lost pets and has had some well-documented successes. After a friend of the website Goop (Gwyneth Paltrow's wellness company Goop) lost her cat, she called Tim. He was able to pinpoint the exact town house in New York City's West Village where the cat was ultimately found alive, two days later, under a floorboard. Quite a feat. He was written up in Goop for his success, and interviewed in a post called "What Your Pets Are Really Thinking."

Tim himself is not what I would call particularly Goop-y, save for his mystical profession—he's a Southerner with a website that looks like a prop in a movie about what the internet was like in the '90s, and an affinity for golf shirts tucked into khakis. (I imagine the standard Goop version of an animal communicator is, like, a muscly, shirtless, long-haired Californian whose slick website doesn't tell you what he does, but does feature him sensually holding a lion, and in a session he tells you he actually needs to touch *you* to communicate with your animal.)

You have to admit that you, too, are wondering how the fuck—excuse me, you're wondering how, exactly, he found that cat.

When he begins the search for a lost pet, he told me he first asks for some basic information about the animal—what they look like, where and when they were last seen, et cetera. ("It's not a guessing game. The more information I have, the better.") Then he "drops to [his] heart center" (that information is becoming very useful) and attempts to reach the animal telepathically, to gain any information about their whereabouts he can—what they see in front of them, what they see above them, what they smell, what they hear, and so on—and then he does a technique called map dowsing.

To map dowse, he pulls out a pendulum and a bunch of maps around the area where the animal was last seen. "The pendulum is connecting with the animal, detecting the energy of where the animal is most likely located, or where the energy is the strongest." It narrows down the area typically within a block or so, sometimes a little farther, sometimes closer. "Occasionally it's exact." The pendulum swings one way when it's picking up the energy; another way when it isn't. "Where it's strongest is the grid, that's the area."

This has led to many successful rescues. Two cats in London (found "more than 6,700 kilometers away" from their owners, says the web-accessible press release), and an eighteen-year-old blind Yorkie in Texas, and that Goop cat from before. But how? "After the successes, even after doing this for fifteen years, I scratch my head," he said. "I have no idea. I have no idea." Damn.

There is no doubt in my mind that, if Peter were lost, I would call Tim and give him any amount of my money to swing a pendulum over a map. I would pay extra for more pendulums, more maps. Like many people, I would do anything.

The cats and dogs aren't always found, though, and communicators are quick to tell you that no communicator is going to be accurate 100 percent of the time. "With some communicators," DelMonte told me, "my clients will tell me, 'Oh they said this, they said that.' And I would never criticize a colleague, but to myself I roll my eyes, like, oh my god...Where the hell did they get that?"

This can be harmful. Many animal communicators offer medical advice (rather, they intuit this medical advice from what the animal is telling them they need), which can get dangerous, particularly when that medical advice goes against the advice of the client's veterinarian.

"When I die, I do not want to go to the veterinarian," reads a transcript from a communication session with a sixteen-year-old dog named Maki on communicator Laura Stinchfield's website. "I don't want to go. I think that I should just go naturally, or someone should come here and shoot me with a dart. Then I want to go naturally. Well if I have to go, I want to have a fresh blanket that smells like our detergent and I want to have mom and dad there and no one else. No one. Ok?"

You can maybe see how something like an old dog apparently arguing against his own euthanasia might make some uneasy. And this is where it gets difficult for me. I think animal communicators, whether or not they actually talk to your dog over the phone, have something important to offer. They want you to know your animal is worth taking interest in and listening to. It is, of course, not a lesson exclusive to animal communication; much of animal science, particularly that focused on animal cognition, aims to tell you the same thing. But not everyone has the patience or desire for evidence. For the animals' sake, I think it's worth attempting to reach the people who just want to feel it, too.

"I'm an animal advocate," Cathy Malkin, the communicator from Pleasant Hill, told me. "I teach people how to be kind and humane to animals, because sometimes we just don't know. A lot of people do things...they don't do it out of malice, they just don't know."

If you were to listen to reason you'd figure that most if not all animal communicators are taking people's money and lying to them. Bilking people who desire something they just cannot have is an unseemly practice, but again it isn't one exclusive to animal communication. I buy a lot of things that promise me an impossibility. Serums to make my skin perfect, products with CBD in them to make me calm, sack-like outfits that only looked good on the tall model. They're ultimately harmless, save for the effect they have on my bank account. But this is not all harmless.

If Peter were sick, I don't think I would go to an animal communicator for a second opinion, because I'm inclined toward skepticism and, frankly, anger in the convergence of woo-woo and medicine. But I just barely wouldn't. Like with buying a map dowsing session for a lost pet, there are situations where a person will do anything if it even slightly increases the possibility of saving the animal they love. Not only is this rotten in the fact that it extracts money from vulnerable people; it can be dangerous for those feeling like medicine is not giving them the result they want.

"Almost 90 percent of the patients I see are very ill," Douglas Palma told me. He's an internal medicine specialist for small animals at the Animal Medical Center in New York City, and I reached out to him to see if he had much experience with owners turning to unconventional sources. "The owners have already seen three or four vets, and their pet has been sick for months now, so they're frustrated. They're willing to believe anyone who gives them any hope." This hope can come in the form of alternative or holistic medicine, or, of course, animal communicators. "They're naturally going to glom onto those things.

"I had a woman the other day—I just did an endoscopy on the dog, and the dog has lymphoma. And according to the animal communicator, the dog had a parasite." Not only did the dog have a parasite, said the animal communicator, but the owner was killing the dog with the food she was feeding him, because the parasite was in the food. The owner took the communicator's diagnosis to heart. "She was actually quite distraught by it," Palma said. "And it really pissed me off. Because I have this woman, and her dog is sick, her dog has lymphoma, and she's got this woman telling her behind the scenes that her dog is sick because of something that she's doing. And she's just trying to help the dog!"

Palma points out that he's not, in general, against all of this woo-woo sort of stuff. Medicine and science are always changing and evolving; what we believe to be true now can be proved false and vice versa. "So I'm open to any and all other things that are out there. But I have not been proven wrong by an animal communicator yet. So that's kind of my stance on it, I guess."

Despite my natural skepticism, I am also open to any and all things and, in fact, own four crystals. So I thought it was time to have our own reading.

My session with the communicator who told me about the brown treats began with a warning that the energy he was about to pick up on could be from my dog, or a friend's dog, or any dog I have seen in the neighborhood, or a dog from my past, or any dog I had seen on television or in a video online. Clearly he had a large pool of dog energy to draw from. He didn't mention fictional dogs, though, so I assume Augie Doggie and Doggie Daddy were out.

I was told to keep my mind open, and to really try to think about whom he might possibly be reaching. (Why it would matter whether or not I could pinpoint the exact wrong dog he was in contact with is a concept that is lost on me, I have to admit. Like, Oh, yeah—that sounds like Jacob from the dog park. How's he doing?)

"I'm seeing a lot of curly hair ... is Peter ... a cockapoo?"

Peter is not a cockapoo.

"Okay, do any of your friends have cockapoos, or a breed like cockapoos?" No. "Has Peter interacted with any cockapoos in the neighborhood?" No. "Are you sure?" Yes. "Are you really thinking—is there any neighborhood cockapoo that you might not be remembering?" No, I truly did not know of a single cockapoo in the neighborhood.

It continued to go about as well as that. "Does he have...a red ball toy?" Although he has a gigantic mountain of toys, he doesn't have a red ball, no. "Oh...actually, okay yes, it's a Kong. Does he have a Kong?" Well, yes, he does have a Kong.

"Is he...about eight years old?" I think he's about five.

"He's saying he really likes...going in the water?" No, I'm sorry, he's actually afraid of going in water, though we did take a trip to the beach once. He stayed on the sand and saw the water, could that be it? "Ah, see, that's it!"

"He's telling me he hates...riding in the car?" Ahh actually, I'm sorry but he really loves riding in the car.

It was very awkward.

Peter, as you know, lives for a car trip. Little Bear, however, hated the car. He was my family's dog, and he died at thirteen years old, about seven years prior to this reading.

I must admit to you now that Little Bear was a cocker spaniel. I know. You're likely wondering why I didn't provide this information when the communicator was looking for something, anything, anything at all, that might link me to a cockapoo, a breed that is a mix of cocker spaniel and poodle. There this communicator was, struggling to get me to see that my dog was apparently trying to talk with me from beyond, and I was being a stubborn asshole about it—why?

Well, first of all, please be nice to me. Okay? So. He told me the cockapoo was tan and Little Bear was black. Plus we kept his hair short, so he wasn't particularly curly except for his ears, so the picture I had in my head of this cockapoo was not Little Bear. And in addition, none of the water stuff or red ball stuff or age stuff lined up, either. Okay?

Mainly, though, I did not want to travel down what I sensed was going to be an emotionally manipulative line of communication. That sort of John Edward style—"Did you have a deceased loved one whose name starts with 'J'? Well, he's in heaven now and he wants you to know he's proud of you." I am too easily swayed by this sort of thing. I need to avoid the temptation to cry over nonsense whenever possible. Still, I couldn't deal with telling the communicator that he was wrong anymore; it was too uncomfortable. Plus, hating the car is truly a trait that stands out in my memory of Little Bear. So I offered it.

"Well, that's who it is! He's telling me yes, yes, it's him!"

Of course, I started crying immediately. I hadn't emotionally prepared myself for *this*. I wasn't living at home when Little Bear died, and I carry around guilt that I wasn't able to say goodbye, and I miss him. There was an obvious difference in speaking to Peter through this communicator and speaking to Little Bear. After we hung up, Peter would still be there.

I wanted to cry over the phone with this stranger who was telling me my dead dog was trying to talk to me about as much as I wanted to have a three-way conversation with him and my dead dog. I had things to say to Little Bear, of course—that I was sorry, that I wished we could have had the kind of relationship Peter and I have rather than that of just a child and a family dog—but not through this strange man. My communication with Little Bear should be private. The communicator, after lightly chastising me for not knowing the tan cockapoo was my dead black cocker spaniel ("he's like, yeah, hello, finally!"), and then telling me a long, involved story about a woman who didn't realize her dead uncle was trying to talk to her even though he had, like, a peg leg or something (a tale I assume was at least in part designed to run out the clock), asked if I had anything to ask Little Bear. God. I don't know. What can you say? I said I wanted to know if he was okay. He told me he was. I said to tell him I loved him. He told me he did.

I left the call drained and heartsick, convinced I'd made Little Bear feel forgotten because I hadn't admitted to the phone man that he could potentially be the dog he was sensing. I still feel horrible about it. I'm not sure if this guy really made contact with my sweet Little Bear, but if he did, I hope that means Little Bear is here and he knows that dude was just giving me a very weird vibe.

I wanted another session. I still wanted to talk to Peter, and ideally I did not want to feel like shit afterward. The next communicator I spoke with was a woman from New York. We began our session, thirty minutes for $95, with a deep breathing meditation to "drop down to our heart centers" (remember?). Then she got to the work of sensing Peter, which she did with relative ease. Is he a small black dog? In fact he is. (Maybe the key to communicating effectively is being slightly vague.)

She laughed at his energy and told me he was sweet, and that she sensed we had a "relaxed codependence," which is a beautiful way of putting it. ("Like, oh yeah, I live with my dog, he's my friend," she said, doing—you have to admit—a pretty good impression of me.) She said he was not an alpha, but rather a "delicate young man." This was one of several things, including the question "do you make art about him? Because he says he's okay with it," that made me slightly nervous she'd read my writing about him in advance of the phone call, though I would never accuse her of such a thing because I loved her and enjoyed our conversation very much.

"He's kind of elitist," she said, but "not particularly neurotic, he just likes things to be proper." This felt true, too. My proper little man. The most surprising part of the phone call came after I asked if there was anything that made Peter feel particularly anxious. She said, "This is weird, because this sort of thing usually comes from neighbors above the ceiling—but I'm seeing something shaking underneath him?" This was a bit spooky because just outside of the street-facing window in my bedroom, where Peter tends to hang out, were a few construction workers who had been jackhammering incessantly for days. I hated them, too, and their stupid, loud construction. I immediately thought she could hear them on the line, but the door to that room was closed and I was two rooms away. It was still possible. But maybe Peter had just...told her?

Finally, she told me she saw me and Peter sitting next to each other in "sort of a glowing heart." The scenery around us changed rapidly, she said—city, country, forest, beach, space—but we just sat there together in it. "Does that sound right?" she asked. It did.

I left the call with the sort of blissed-out feeling one gets from spending twelve dollars on a single cup of juice.

It's difficult to feel a deep connection with an animal, like I do with Peter, and completely discount the idea that there might be people out there with the ability to access a similar but deeper one. People who have a preternatural ability for communion; a Michael Jordan–level talent for empathy. And it seems to me that, with animals, there is more of an opportunity to use that natural inclination for good rather than manipulation, by which I mean expertly guessing your way through a conversation about someone's dead human loved one for cash. Your animals feel things; they have needs, they have desires, they are whole creatures who want to be understood. The communicator's message is, at least, a good one. I just can't quite bring myself to disavow them altogether.

But should we go as far as to take a communicator's word on the non-veterinarian-approved sources of our dogs' illnesses, as well as our dogs' apparent opinions regarding the function of euthanasia? Well. Let me drop down to my heart center and attempt to communicate to you what I'm thinking.

Can you sense it?

Chapter 11

CAN DOGS HUNT GHOSTS?

I hope Peter haunts me after he dies. God, that would be great. I wouldn't need much—I don't need to be able to see a gauzy version of him or anything, but I'd like to be able to sense his presence. Maybe feel him shift on the couch, or get the sensation of a nose on my shoulder in bed, asking me to lift the covers so he could burrow underneath. Maybe hear a little ghostly groan if he was bothered too much by my affection.

At home things would be essentially the same as they are now, I think, save for his corporeal presence. But if his spirit were attached to me (rather than attached to the apartment; I'm not sure how it works) I could bring him everywhere. To museums, on airplanes. We'd be able to "eat" together at restaurants, and I could take him to the doctor with me so that his gentle ghostly nature might soothe me. I'd have to decide whether I told other people about him, though. I wouldn't want to keep him a secret, but it's safe to assume some people wouldn't believe me, or would think the "crazy dog lady" got even crazier post-dog. But secrets are hard to keep. Someone might try to sit on him and I'd have to say—DON'T SIT THERE! And then they would naturally want to know why. Or his wagging ghost tail would kick up a little ghostly breeze and someone would be like, "Why does it feel like a little breeze just happened, as if from a happy dog's tail?"

It would be nice to be free from the preoccupation with his death, too, since it will have already happened. That would be a benefit. "I love you," I'd say to ghost Peter. He wouldn't say anything back, since he's a dog and also a ghost, but I think the simple fact of a dog's presence often translates to a feeling of love, and I think I would feel that. I'm trying to think about it and I really don't see any downsides to being haunted by a Peter ghost.

A human ghost would be much worse, though. One night in our old apartment, while we were sleeping in bed, Peter perked up out of a sweet slumber, throwing his body clumsily and violently to the side in order to sit upright. It always scares me when he does this, because I assume it means we're being approached by a living murderer, but I guess if that were the case I would at least be grateful for the heads-up. He sat up in bed and looked toward my open bedroom door; near my door was a mirror (scary: Bloody Mary, vampires) and my acoustic guitar (scary: high school boys who liked Dave

Matthews Band, people who want attention at parties). I said nothing, fearful of an intruder, living or otherwise. Moments later my guitar made a noise—ping! Ah!

I was genuinely frightened.

Was the noise due to the tuning pegs on the guitar shifting, because at that point I left it out of its case at all times, and almost always with the window open no matter the weather? Or was it, oh my god, something more like—*a ghost*?

It would make sense that Peter had noticed him, if it were a ghost. Many believers in paranormal phenomena tend to think dogs' heightened senses allow them to see, or hear, or smell things that we just can't. Ghost hunter Zak Bagans has ghost hunted with his dog named Ridley, a Yorkshire terrier, on his Travel Channel show *Ghost Adventures*, for example. Did I try several times to get him to talk to me for this chapter, going through several sources, and getting slightly close only once? Like with many ghost-related things, you'll never know for sure. "I'm teaching Ridley how to hunt ghosts," Bagans told PEOPLEPets.com in 2010. "He's good. I tried to see if he's sensitive to spiritual energy, and I think he is."

For those interested in training their own dogs in ghost hunting, there's an interesting webpage last updated in 2008 called "How to Train Your Dog to Be a Professional Ghost Hunter," written by a woman named Cheryl Edmond. She ghost hunted with her rottweiler, Stanley. She says that another reason why ghost hunters bring along their dogs is that many ghosts were fearful of dogs in life (though she notes there is no reason to be) and they remain fearful of them in death, causing them to freeze in terror, and therefore become able to be spotted by ghost hunting equipment more easily. It does sound helpful.

To train your dog to hunt ghosts, she advises you to take your dog to a place known to be haunted and keep him on a loose leash, so he's able to dart at any ghost he might come across. You are to move slowly and give him an instruction like, "Find the ghost." She writes that a good place to practice finding ghosts is a funeral, or a place where someone has recently died. That idea checks out to me. "I'm so sorry for your loss," you can practice saying. "Well, anyway, my dog and I would really appreciate if we could try and hunt your wife's ghost while she's fresh." Once you think your dog has spotted a ghost—if he's reacting wildly, going crazy for the ghost— you can take readings with your ghost hunting equipment and confirm. Then, of course, you offer him a treat.

If dogs are able to hunt ghosts, I assume Peter would naturally be a very good ghost hunter. He's very sensitive, and he has good hearing. He has a strong heart and he's very brave. Plus he noticed that my guitar was going to make a ping that one time, you remember. My issue, though, is that I'd rather not make him attempt to hunt any dead human strangers. I'm protective of him, and if he's going to be meeting ghostly humans I'd like a chance to get to know them first, to see if they're nice and worthy of his company. I thought that we should instead seek out a nice dog ghost.

I know one story of a dog ghost, but it's a scary one. (I don't want to go ahead and tell it to you without adequately preparing you.) It's about a dog ghost who "lives" on South Mountain in Maryland, the northernmost section of the Blue Ridge Mountain range. I know his description from the book *Haunted Houses of Harpers Ferry*, by Stephen D. Brown. Maryland residents know him as the "Snarly Yow," and he's said to haunt the mountains, scaring residents because he is very large, has big snarling teeth and red eyes, and is incorporeal. In one story about him a frightened man comes upon the large dog and, scared, throws a rock at him—and it goes right through him. That'll show you for throwing a rock at a dog. In another story a guy comes across the Snarly Yow and tries to shoot a gun at him! His bullets, again, only go right through him. In yet another, kids throw bricks at the ghost dog. You have to wonder why all of these people are so comfortable throwing things at a large animal. Perhaps that's why they're being haunted by the Snarly Yow in the first place.

In my quest to find Peter a less menacing ghost friend, I reached out to Boroughs of the Dead, a company that does ghostly walking tours of New York City, to see if they knew of any dog-related hauntings we might be able to investigate. "It's definitely a gray area," they said. "There is a story that FDR used to walk his dog Fala through Washington Square Park and that Fala's ghost is still there. However, as far as we know, that story was made up by Dr. Phil Schoenberg of Ghosts of New York." They said that if I could prove that story had a "non–Dr. Phil provenance" they'd "love to hear about it!"

My personal sixth sense was ignited—the sense of niche professional New York City ghostly tour group related drama.

I hesitate to bore you with history, but I'd like to give you a brief introduction to Fala. He was a little black Scottish terrier, a Christmas gift to Franklin D. Roosevelt from his cousin Margaret Suckley. Roosevelt loved Fala very much, and took him everywhere. He went to meetings with him, he slept in his bed at night. Roosevelt focused a 1944 campaign speech on him after Republicans accused him of sending a navy destroyer to pick Fala up in the Aleutian Islands, costing taxpayers $20 million. Roosevelt disputed the claim, saying Fala was never left in the Aleutian Islands to begin with.

"I am accustomed to hearing malicious falsehoods about myself, such as that old, worm-eaten chestnut that I have represented myself as indispensable," Roosevelt said in the speech. "But I think I have a right to resent, to object to libelous statements about my dog." There is a statue of Fala at the Franklin Delano Roosevelt Memorial in Washington, DC, and he's buried only a few yards away from the president and First Lady.

Over the phone, Dr. Phil told me about the ghost of Fala. He agreed, first, that dogs are very sensitive to the presence of ghosts, and—though he first clarified that he, himself, doesn't necessarily believe in ghosts—he advised me not to wear any perfume on my ghost hunting trip with Peter to ensure the smell doesn't confuse him. I was grateful for this tip. According to the ghostly tale, Eleanor Roosevelt walked Fala in Washington Square Park when she lived at 29 Washington Square West in the late '40s, after FDR's death. "It is said" (in the story told to me by Dr. Phil) that FDR took him out in Washington Square Park, too; I cannot find further evidence of the claim, but I choose to believe it.

Hunting for drama, I asked how he heard that Fala's ghost was a Washington Square Park resident, particularly considering the fact that he didn't believe in ghosts himself. Dr. Phil told me he heard the rumor from "people talking about it, interviewing people." I pressed further—so they contact you when they see this dog ghost? He said some yeah, and some people spot the dog when they're on his tour. "And they tell you about it right then?" I asked. "Yeah." Perhaps not as strong in my sixth sense as I previously imagined, and lacking the lack of social skills necessary to be a good reporter, I dropped the inquisition.

Washington Square Park is considered to be quite haunted even beyond Fala, because it was used as a mass grave in the late 1700s, and human remains were discovered as recently as 2015 when the city began work installing a water main. Because of this it seemed like Peter and I might be risking a human ghost sighting, but I bet it's hard if not impossible to find a place haunted exclusively by dog ghosts. If there are ghosts, you have to imagine there are a lot of all sorts of them—horses, pigeons, humans, Fala. We would have to take our chances.

In preparation for our ghost hunt, I sought out ghost hunting equipment for purchase online. I'm not sure if you've had much experience attempting to buy ghost hunting equipment, but it turns out much of it is pretty expensive. I'm not sure why I expected otherwise. I guess out of rudeness, as I was considering it to be kind of a joke, but it is in fact not a joke and instead it is very serious and often costs $300. There are special ghost hunting video cameras, special ghost hunting audio recorders, special ghost hunting electromagnetic field (EMF) readers, a special $15 gray ghost hunting hat that says I'D RATHER BE GHOST HUNTING in plain uppercase white letters that I in fact did buy and now love. It's really good. ("IT'S MY HAT!" I said to my boyfriend when the package arrived. I'd previously explained to him that it was really good. "That actually *is* good," he said after he saw the hat, so you know you can trust me about how good it is, particularly if you're someone who believes a man's word over a woman's and now you're caught.)

I bought an EMF meter, too, for $32.97. This is the one piece of ghost hunting equipment you should buy if you can buy only one piece. I know this from ghost hunting TV shows. If you also know this from ghost hunting TV shows, it may shock you to learn that EMF meters were not originally developed with the intent of hunting ghosts; they're meant to detect problems with electrical wiring, and harmful radiation coming from power lines or devices in your home. Lucky for us, they just happen to also detect—ghosts. Ah! Before our hunt I tested it in my apartment; it indeed worked, and I was frightened to find that there is a ghost in my air purifier.

Even with their non-ghostly origins, most of the meters available for sale on Amazon mention ghost hunting explicitly in their descriptions; the one I bought says it's "for Testing Ghost, Magnetic Field, Electric Field Radiation and Ambient Temperature." Two of its displayed customer questions are ghost-related: "Can it detect ghosts?" and "Does dis really help if u trying found out do u have ghost n your house." The answer to both (paraphrasing) is yes.

In addition to Peter and the EMF detector, I added a third tool to my ghost hunting arsenal: a ghost hunter app for my phone that cost 99 cents—an absolute steal. It has many features that I am not going to explain (EVP, FFT-V, Geo-scope Instrument, P-EVP, Sensor Sweep Instrument, Spatial Instrument, Twilight Instrument) but suffice it to say they are all neon green and blinky and serve to tell you if there is a ghost. Actually, I'll explain the EVP, because it is my favorite of the bunch; it stands for "electronic voice phenomena" and it allegedly transcribes words ghosts are saying that are being picked up by my phone somehow. It says things like this: *Pencil. Jerry. Blanket. Soda.* It's perfect. *Pants. Lemon. Jessica. Bag.*

With this final addition to our arsenal, we were ready. Peter and I traveled to Washington Square Park one horrifically chilly morning in February with our tools to find Fala and hopefully no one else. The night before, I'd shown him a photograph of Fala on the internet. "This is the dog you're going to be looking for," I told him. "He's going to be maybe see-through, but I think this will be the general idea." It was Peter's first trip to Manhattan, and I was so excited for him. Finally, a chance to be around an overwhelming number of New York University students. The sight of the park's iconic arch excited him immediately. Though it was just around 7:00 a.m. (I wanted him to avoid the distraction of avant-garde artists, if possible) there were already several dogs there, running around in the park's two off-leash areas and relieving themselves on the grass. Was Fala in the mix? Only time would tell.

I turned on my EMF detector and put it in my pocket, where I could both hear it and see its flashing light if it detected any EMF. At first Peter decided to investigate the park's inner perimeter. He sniffed around, stopping frequently to urinate. Every once in a while he would stop to look up at me as if attempting to communicate either, "Can you believe we're in a new place?" or, "There is a ghost here." I dutifully checked the meter, which never made a sound or registered anything even once, even though I paid over thirty dollars for it and would have preferred it did something so I could note it in this chapter. I kept my eye out for Fala, as well. *Where would a ghost dog be?* I wondered. *A bench?* I couldn't see him on a bench. *Near the, um, arch?* I couldn't see him there, either.

Still not getting any activity on my EMF, I allowed Peter to lead me around the park. He led me into a grassy area, where he continued to sniff and urinate. All part of his process. As a dog exited the off-leash park to our right, designated for smaller dogs, all at once he seemed to have caught a scent. At last! He dragged me over to the entrance, pulling excitedly on his leash, seeming to point to the location right outside the park's gate. Again, he sniffed wildly. He lifted his leg to urinate, which at this point was just a clever ruse, and "urinated." I scanned for EMF. My stupid thing was not picking up any EMF, even though I was sure some EMF must have been around. I pivoted to my app and scanned for EVP. After about two minutes elapsed, we—yes!—had some voice phenomena to interpret:

Junius
Scary
Lloyd
Karen
Ryan

Hm. I have to say the voice phenomena provided was even harder to crack than I anticipated. What was Fala trying to tell us? Let's see. Junius was the pseudonym of an eighteenth-century writer, which is what I am. So okay, that one checks out. Scary...well, yes, it was a scary activity we were doing. Lloyd? I feel maybe the EVP potentially misheard the name Fala was trying to communicate, which may have been: Franklin Delano Roosevelt. (Delalloyd, perhaps, is what it thought it heard.) Karen, ah...it does have a similar vibe to Eleanor. And Ryan, I guess, must have been another ghost trying to tell us about the swimmer Ryan Lochte.

Peter pulled me back onto the grass—the spirit had moved him once again, or actually, no, my apologies, something else did. For the sake of his privacy we don't need to get into what it was.

One of the nice things about doing a reporting activity like this with a dog is that you can call it a day pretty quickly, because it's cold, and your dog doesn't want to be out here hunting ghosts forever. But we did have one more stop to make.

There were a few other ghostly sights within walking distance of the park. Edgar Allan Poe lived at 85 West 3rd Street, now part of the NYU School of Law, for a few months in 1844. It's reportedly where he wrote "The Cask of Amontillado" and part of "The Raven," and his ghost has been sighted there climbing the banister. I would have hoped better for old Poe than to have to spend eternity at NYU, but I suppose that we can't choose our final haunting places. Across the street at 84 West 3rd Street, the ghost of a fire-fighter allegedly haunts an old fire station now converted into a private residence. He hanged himself in 1930 after finding out his wife had cheated on him, and now he just has to be there forever I guess. Damn. I really do feel you should be able to choose your location.

Of course, these ghosts are too spooky for Peter. I don't want him to have to encounter a sad guy, or a literary critic. He has it hard enough already, having only his mouth to pick up all of his items rather than dexterous paws. Luckily for us, there was one more stop nearby haunted by many old specters: memories and demons, seasons and cities. The jazz man, and the performance artist who was also a waiter, if you remember him. One place where the intense emotion lives on, in a dimension just beyond our own.

Carrie Bradshaw's stoop from the HBO series *Sex and the City*.

The iconic stoop is mere blocks away from Washington Square Park, at 66 Perry Street, and it is a tourist destination so popular that it is decorated with signs begging you to please go away and never come back for the love of god. And I know what you're thinking. "No, Kelly. Carrie's apartment isn't where the ghosts are. *Miranda's* apartment was the one that had the ghost; Carrie was only 'haunted' (in the ghost episode, which was season four, episode five, 'Ghost Town') by feelings for Aidan stirred by the grand opening of Steve's bar," and you're right. But I'd like you to remember that we're primarily looking for dog ghosts.

In terms of dogs on *Sex and the City*, it seems to me that Aidan's dog Pete would be the one most driven to haunt this earthly plane, seeking revenge against Carrie Bradshaw, who lost him—her boyfriend's dog, the boyfriend she *had been cheating on*—in season three, episode ten ("All or Nothing") while she was outside talking to her paramour Big. And I don't want to be morbid, but the seasons in which Pete was featured aired from 2000 to 2002. I have to imagine Pete has, at this point, passed on. He is missed. And if his spirit is still with us, he is there on that stoop, forever waiting for Carrie to come back, so he can tell her to eat shit.

Pete was a beautiful Brittany spaniel, and while we stood looking at Carrie's stoop I attempted to communicate his image to Peter, so he could know which dog he was looking for. I dropped down to my heart center, if you remember that. I showed him Pete in my mind. That they have the same name, I assumed, would lead more easily to a connection. I watched Peter for any signs that he was sensing something ghostly. He sniffed around. He looked up at me with a face that seemed to ask, "Why are we standing here?" His ears were regular. I didn't even get the sense that he recognized the stoop from when we'd watched *Sex and the City* together. Perhaps, I noted, we would have to watch much more *Sex and the City* when we got home.

I brought out my phone to take a quick EVP reading and noticed that my battery was dropping at an alarming rate. Was this because iPhones perform spectacularly badly in cold weather to a degree that is absolutely insane, like, what are we even paying for, are we just not supposed to be able to use our phones outside in the winter? Or was it because of the ghost of Pete? I cannot say for sure. I quickly scanned for voice phenomena and after a few moments a word appeared and it was, I swear to Fala: "Tramp." Was Pete slut shaming Carrie?

Seconds later my phone died.

Peter and I took a taxi home and I made him a scrambled egg to add to his kibble as a reward for his bravery. I had a scrambled egg, too, as a reward for mine. Had Fala's spirit attached himself to us, to "live" with us forever as our new ghost dog friend? Well. I think it's as likely as anything else.

Chapter 12

CAN I ACCEPT THAT MY DOG WILL NEVER BE A DANCER?

In 2018 Maria Konnikova, an experimental psychologist and *New Yorker* contributing writer, made the surprising decision to delay work on a book she was writing about the confluence of skill and chance. The book looked at the phenomenon through the lens of poker, and in researching the game, Konnikova became good at it—too good. She started winning tournaments, bringing in sponsorships and big money. The book was left in the dust while she juiced her newfound moneymaking skill; a talent she, until that point, didn't even know she possessed.

This is not a similar story.

I'd been vaguely interested in ballet for a handful of years when I decided to transfer any hope I had for my dance career onto Peter. Yes, being vaguely interested in something for a handful of years sounds like an indisputable recipe for relatively late-in-life success, but the truth is that I was not very good. Although I'd taken a total of three six-week courses of Adult Beginner Ballet I at a local dance studio, I had yet to graduate into Adult Beginner Ballet II.

Admittedly the only thing required to move onto Adult Beginner Ballet II is having taken Adult Beginner Ballet I, but I never thought I'd learned the basics well enough to make the *changement* (a ballet term). There was no test, but I know I couldn't pass it if there were, and I saw no point in putting myself through the humiliation of failing to blend in with a slightly more advanced group of adult beginners. My main problem is arm-related. I just don't know how to do them. The feet, moving them around...I can pretty much do that, at least in terms of what is required of a person enrolled in Adult Beginner Ballet I. Things like pointing the toe and sliding it on the floor in front of you. Pointing the toe and putting it behind you. Raising the toe to your opposite leg. But the addition of the arms I can't handle. Holding them out in a pizza in front of you while moving your toe around. Taking a leap to the left while raising them in a moon over your head. It was too much. Plus I have a suspicion that mine just don't bend the right sort of way, or that I maybe have an excess of bones.

Peter, on the other hand, is breathtakingly graceful. It is a pleasure to watch him lift his leg to urinate—so poised, with such control. At once strong and delicate. A perfect ballerino; a dog Mikhail Baryshnikov. Yes, he'll sometimes take a stumble if the floor is too clean and he is too excited about the fact that it's dinnertime, but who among us does not sometimes fall out of sheer exuberance. Overall he is quite nimble.

His main dance-related talent is spinning. He's a natural spinner, and will do it over and over, like a cartoon, whenever he's excited about anything—a walk, a drive, playtime, dinnertime, the sound of a bag crinkling, the sense that someone, somewhere is picking up a fork. Leaning into his natural abilities, I taught him "spin" as a trick one day in our apartment. I led him into a spin with a piece of carrot, and then said, "SPIN," and gave him the carrot. I led him into a spin with a piece of carrot, and then said, "SPIN," and gave him the carrot. I led him into a spin with a piece of carrot, and then said, "SPIN," and gave him the carrot. It took maybe two minutes before he could spin on command. I know what you're thinking—*holy shit . . . this dog seems to be genius-level at spinning.* And you're right.

Clearly we had to put his talent to use.

I came across canine freestyle while browsing through "dancing dog" viral videos on YouTube very late one night, and please don't pretend you haven't done it yourself, I know that you have and that I am not alone. "Salsa Dog" is a good one, but have you seen "Dancing Merengue Dog"? Oh, you haven't lived until you've seen "Dancing Merengue Dog." The video shows a golden retriever doing what can only be described as a suspiciously impressive dance routine with a man, each of them dressed in salsa-style clothing, in front of a small crowd of people in, for some reason, a parking lot, who are, sure, delighted to see the dance, but not nearly as delighted as they should be—not nearly as delighted as the dance deserves. They are clapping, but they are not weeping. They are laughing, but where are the Beatlemania-style screams?

The video lasts for three minutes. The dog stands on her hind legs, spinning, hopping, and moving backward and forward with the man to the rhythm. The man takes her hand and spins her several times. She has the standard happy look of a golden retriever but her vibe vacillates between "I am feeling the music and am in complete control!" and "an outside force is controlling my body and I don't know what is going on, please help!" It has an emotional arc similar to that of a joke that goes on for too long, and then goes on so much longer that it becomes funny again.

The recommended videos for those watching "Dancing Merengue Dog" included several from "canine freestyle" competitions, mostly from the Crufts dog show, an annual international dog competition in England featuring the sort of "best in show" breed crowning that you'd expect from any dog show, as well as competitions in agility, obedience, and canine freestyle. I had not heard of canine freestyle until that night. In a moment, my life—and now yours by association—changed irreparably.

Do you know about canine freestyle? Please allow me to explain. It is dancing with a dog. That's essentially it. An outgrowth of obedience, the sport requires a human to choreograph a routine of tricks for a dog to perform with her to a chosen song. There are costumes (almost always on the human, less often on the dog) and props. Participants are judged on timing and flair, and on how discreetly their dogs are instructed to perform their tricks. It should be imperceptible—a flick of the hand, a nudge of the head, a telepathic connection brought to life by the spirit of rhythmic movement; ideally the command will blend in as part of the human's dancing. The effect should be fluid, as if the two are performing of their own volition. It is the most artistic and relaxed of the dog sports, hence the "freestyle" in the name. (It is also known as freestyle heelwork.) It is the sort of thing that makes you happy to be alive, rather than all the time wanting to be a dead skeleton in the dirt.

It's incredibly touching to watch a human in a sparkly tuxedo debase herself in front of a crowd so that her dog might have a moment in the sun. And the dogs truly seem to have fun, running, spinning, hopping onto their dance partner's feet as they waddle for a few steps. Leaping over their partner's sparkly dance cane. No doubt the result of many Saturdays spent getting to the studio at 8:00 a.m., turning on the boombox, listening to Dave Brubeck's "Take Five" four hundred times, and attempting to get a dog to hop on cue, all to produce a deeply strange little moment. It's beautiful.

One video in particular makes me cry every time I see it. (Though, "every time I see it" makes it sound like I come upon it by happenstance—really, it makes me cry every time I seek it out specifically to trigger this emotional response.) It's from the 2018 Crufts dog show, and features a young woman, Emma, and her sheepdog, Yola, dancing to the musician Ruth B.'s 2015 song "Lost Boy," which you might recognize from the smooth-café-themed satellite radio station set to play permanently in my parents' car. The melancholy-sounding song is told from the viewpoint of a Lost Boy saved by his friendship with Peter Pan. Emma is dressed like Peter Pan; Yola is mercifully without a costume.

Yola weaves through Emma's legs and leaps over her arms; they move in sync around the competition turf while Ruth B. sings about the promise of never feeling lonely again. At one point Yola puts her arms around Emma's neck, and the two pretend to fly together. In her final move, as the song ends, Yola rolls herself into a blanket and pretends to go to sleep. If you must know, I'm weeping as I type this to you.

I am, I realize, potentially too emotional for canine freestyle.

Still, we had to do it. Watching the dogs dance, I had an immediate flash of inspiration: the darkroom scene from the 1957 classic film *Funny Face*. I would be Fred Astaire and Peter, naturally, would be Audrey Hepburn. It would be perfect. He's already dressed in her iconic, all-black *Funny*

Face outfit, as if he were born to play the role. And true, yes, that's not the outfit she wears in the darkroom scene—the darkroom scene is the scene in which they sing "Funny Face," the song we'd use in our routine—but an artist's job is not to focus on what will or will not go over the audience's head. An artist's job is to create. The audience and judges would just have to figure out for themselves the fact that Peter's all-black fur was intended as a reference to Audrey Hepburn's outfit in the bohemian dance scene from later in the movie.

I immediately ordered an instructional book online—from what retailer? A delicious secret for me to keep—called *Dancing with Dogs*. I knew I would love it from a note highlighted in one of its first pages:

DOG COSTUMES: When dressing up a dog, stick to a simple collar or neckwear so the dignity of the dog is maintained.

Indeed. The book meticulously lays out the steps a human must take to build their dog's cache of tricks with easy language and helpful, adorable photos, before launching into the good stuff—the routines. Titled things like "singing in the rain" (a routine that uses an umbrella as a prop, inviting your dog to hop over it, walk between your legs, and twirl with you while you're twirling with the umbrella), "puppet on a string" (in this one you're the puppeteer and your dog is the puppet; you move him in a figure-8 formation as if controlling him by a wooden dowel), and "viva España" (I'm going to pass the description of this one on to the book: "The end of this Spanish bullfighting routine is cunningly choreographed to ensure that the bull gets his revenge by killing the matador!") (I can't tell you how much I love this book), there is a sequence of tricks for every taste, accompanied, again, by delightful photos of dogs and humans engaged in joyous dance: humans in ridiculous costume, dogs fully nude. I was desperate to start, but found the book to not be particularly suited to my rebellious attitude. I just can't learn from a book; anything with a hint of school makes me tune out, fail, and listen to anarcho-punk as if it actually sounds good.

(*Maybe that was your problem with ballet?* you're aptly thinking, and it was, but also my problem with ballet was my arms and legs.)

The book came with a forward from the founder and president of the World Canine Freestyle Organization, which I found out was headquartered—oh my god—this was actually shocking, I'm not kidding—about a twenty-minute drive from my apartment. It was fate! I emailed the address provided on the site and asked if they offered lessons, and she emailed me back herself to tell me that they did, and to give her a call.

It seemed the world had a plan for us.

I called and she told me that she offered lessons herself, for $45 an hour; an absolutely reasonable sum, and one I was happy to pay. She asked what sort of level Peter was at currently in terms of tricks, and I told her that he could sit and stay, and that, of course—as she may have heard—he's genius-level at spinning, but that was pretty much the extent of it. She told me to teach him "watch," "wait," and "come." "Take his favorite treat, tiny bits," she said, "put it right in front of his nose, and say, 'Watch!'" This command allows the dog to focus attention on the human in order to receive instruction. To teach "wait," she said to make him wait before eating his dinner. "Come" comes after he can wait. When he knew those tricks, I was to call her back and set up a lesson.

Over the next month, we went to work. "WATCH!" I'd say, holding a treat to my nose. "WATCH!" He learned them all pretty quickly, as if the knowledge already resided in him and I was merely refreshing his memory, but I wanted to be sure he knew them perfectly before we began our study. So we practiced, and practiced. "Waaaaiit..." I'd say while he sat in front of his bowl, waiting, refusing to look in the direction of his food, so that, I assume, the possibility would not be too tempting. "Waaaaait...waaaaaaaait...okay!"

Once I was confident, I called WCFO's founder back. She was traveling and asked me to call back in a few weeks. In a few weeks I called back; she still couldn't do it. After some time passed, I emailed. Nothing. Desperately I emailed a few more times—*not to bother you but just checking in, ha-ha!* Months passed.

My kismet was dying.

I'm not sure what happened—I suspect she could tell we were going to be major players in the world of canine freestyle and she was afraid of the competition—but eventually I had to move on. I reached out to Amanda, our agility instructor (we'd taken our entire course of agility lessons in the time that elapsed) to see if she had any experience teaching freestyle, and she said she did not, but that she'd taken a few classes in the sport and could get us started with a few tricks. Perfect. We were sort of back on track.

Peter and I headed back to Doggie Academy, and he could not contain his excitement. He spun and spun and looked at me with wild eyes and mouth agape—*Could it be true? Could this really be happening?* It can, my friend.

Back in the room, we discovered something about our respective talents in canine freestyle that was similar to what we'd discovered about our respective talents in canine agility: I was immediately not good at it, Peter was perfect, and Amanda was not shy in pointing this out.

"It would help if you were flexible," she said, as I stood with my legs very far apart, like an awkward triangle, in an effort to allow Peter to weave through them. It's true that would have helped. It would have also helped if I were coordinated. She instructed me to coax Peter under one leg with a treat in the hand opposite to that leg, then switch treat hands and coax him back under the other leg until he returned to his starting point. Or maybe the treat began in the same hand as the leg? I can't remember, which is a lie, I actually never knew, but whatever it was, it was incredibly difficult. I am not made for dancing. It feels like body math. Amanda showed me how to do it first with her dog, a tiny white fluffy girl, and then with Peter, and, indeed, the problem was not Peter.

"Anything he's doing wrong is because of what you're doing," she said, as if I could not already tell that very clearly. Amanda, I get it. Though she didn't know of anyone local, she gave me the name of a woman who could continue our lessons via online video chat. It would have to do.

In the meantime, I figured I should take in some canine freestyle in the flesh. The sport is not nearly as popular as it should be, and the closest event within the next few months took place in Red Lion, Pennsylvania, a three-hour drive away. The drive might have discouraged me, but the event's name called to me like a siren: "Dancing Away Again…in Bark-A-Ritaville."

Dancing Away Again…in Bark-A-Ritaville started at 9:00 a.m., so I left around 5:45 a.m. (without Peter, as only competing dogs were allowed inside the building) and drove, and drove, and drove.

I plainly stood out in Bark-A-Ritaville. The other attendees were uniformly not only attendees but participants, and each of them had a dog and was clearly dressed for their routine, in sparkly outfits or suspenders or coattails. "You're missing your partner!" a man called out to me in the parking lot. "Oh, I'm just here to watch!" I said, noting in real time that the interaction sounded perverted.

The room, a dog obedience and agility gym, was large and open with about thirty humans and their dogs seated in three rows, facing an area roped off and designated as the stage, flanked on one side by three judges. The floor was soft and blue, and every wall was covered floor-to-ceiling in photos of champion dogs and their competition ribbons. Near the entrance was a table with a sign that read WELCOME TO BARK-A-RITAVILLE! and three bowls, designated FOR WHENEVER YOU NEED A LIFT (full of candy), FOR YOUR DOGS (treats), and FOR YOU TO RELIEVE ANY STRESS (stress balls in the shape of dog paws). Next to it hung a large piece of paper—a BOARD OF AFFIRMATIONS—inviting everyone to share what their dog had done well that day. Between competitions, there would be a potluck lunch.

Standing alone in the large, open space, suspiciously without a dog, suspiciously a stranger, and suspiciously about twenty years younger than any other human in attendance, I was greeted by Deb. Palpably confused as to why I would be there, but excited that I for some reason wanted to be, she helpfully told me she'd grab me a chair. I assumed she would add it to one of the three already-formed rows, but Deb had other plans in mind; instead she placed my chair in front of them all, right in front of the stage, alone. My own row. The spectator's row.

I do hope you get to attend a canine freestyle event at some point. Whether the dogs do well or simply run around the ring as their music plays, completely unable to be reined in by their human, as one dog did on two separate tries, it is just joyous. My favorite team, though I do believe they had an unfair advantage, was a group of two golden retrievers and one woman. They had a great move, where the woman would place her hands on her hips and the golden retrievers would stick their big heads into her arm holes. Just delightful. I joined a group of the participants, all locals, talking after the performances were complete, and they encouraged me to keep studying dance with my dog, and where was I from again? Brooklyn? Brooklyn, New York? And I came all the way here *for this*? And I had.

My video freestyle lesson was more successful than I imagined it would be. My instructor's name was Jenn: a certified professional dog trainer and competitive canine freestyle participant. I was worried about the at-home lesson because whenever Peter senses I want him to do something strange—let me brush his teeth, let me give him a bath—he runs into his crate in fear. I assumed he'd feel some anxiety about trick-learning and pull the same self-protective maneuver during our class, and he absolutely did, but not particularly often. We focused on getting Peter to spin in the opposite direction, which we called "TWIST!," and he seemed to be getting it. Then we changed tack and attempted to get him to walk under my leg when I pointed my toe in front of me. *Ah, toe-pointing*, I thought. *I know a little something about this.* In fact, I did not. I watched myself do it, and then I watched Jenn do it—she looked like a ballerina; I looked like someone whose leg had recently fallen asleep and was momentarily not within their control. Could I maybe point my toe with a little more authority? she asked. Peter would benefit from being more clearly instructed.

We accomplished a lot in the one-hour session, and I immediately booked another.

During the next week, Peter and I stayed for a few days with my boyfriend, Chris, in Queens. I'm not sure if you're familiar with the geography of New York City, but although my section of Brooklyn and his section of Queens are only about fourteen miles apart, we are essentially in a long-distance relationship that requires planning and packing and telling friends things like, "No, I can't, sorry. I'm in Queens this weekend."

On Tuesday morning, Chris offered to take Peter to the off-leash park. I didn't go. This is one of the things I keep thinking about. I think, *I should have gone, why didn't I go?* I didn't go because I was in pajamas, because I was going to clean up and make breakfast, or whatever. Because I was lazy. Because it's nice to let someone else do a dog-related chore for you, even if thinking about it as a chore, particularly now, makes you feel like a monster. Of course if nothing had happened it would have been forgotten; a nice, unremarkable thing. I wouldn't be thinking, *I should have gone, why didn't I go?* I wouldn't be thinking anything.

At some point, I picked up my phone noticed that I'd missed a call from Chris. A bad sign. I called him back and he didn't answer. A worse one. He got back a few tense minutes later and told me Peter had gotten hurt, he was running and started to yelp; he couldn't pick up my call because he was carrying him back. While he explained, I checked Peter for blood and there wasn't any; he had all of his limbs, his head was fine, his ears were fine, his paws were fine, his tail was there. How many yelps? Just one or more than one? He said more than one, a few. What happened? He was running and then stopped and yelped and started to limp. Did he get caught in something? There was nothing, there wasn't a hole, there weren't dogs around him, there wasn't any glass beneath him. He was limping, stoically; holding his front left paw in the air without showing signs of distress other than that he was clearly afraid.

Chris has his own dog, a shepherd mix named Frank. He and Frank are similar—open, happy, good-natured, easy to be around, outdoorsy. Learning their similarities served to highlight, for me, mine and Peter's: We are quiet and reserved, goofy when comfortable, loving and fiercely protective. We're appreciative of the outdoors to an extent. We're light sleepers. Chris and Frank are the dog-and-human pair I know best other than me and Peter, and I wonder if all dogs and humans feel paired up so accurately. Peter is mine. There is no doubt about it. And he was in pain.

Chris's vet goes by the nom de vétérinaire "Dr. Pet Daddy." This was amusing to me until Dr. Pet Daddy was the one putting a muzzle on Peter so that he could manipulate his damaged arm without fear of being bitten while Peter loudly squealed, looking at me pleadingly, *Why are you letting this happen, what is happening?* I so badly wanted Dr. Pet Daddy to stop. This pain seemed needless. Something was obviously wrong, and he needed an X-ray; couldn't we just skip this part? What was this for? I held Peter's little face in my hands sobbing, unable to hold it together for him, saying I'm sorry, I'm sorry, I'm sorry, I'm sorry.

After taking him for an X-ray, Dr. Pet Daddy reentered the exam room. "Well, it's not good news," he said. Thanks a lot, Dr. Pet Daddy.

The X-ray showed that Peter had broken his elbow and would need surgery to fix it. From Mikhail Baryshnikov to Nancy Kerrigan. "Why," indeed. There was some scar tissue around the break, and Dr. Pet Daddy said it looked like the bone had suffered trauma in the past and had tried to heal by itself, but couldn't. It was something like a stress fracture. It was weak and it just finally broke. Or, well, this was one theory. Another was that Peter could have cancer. "I just don't know why this would have happened in a healthy dog," Dr. Pet Daddy said.

"I just don't know why this would have happened in a healthy dog," my vet said later, too. Couldn't it just be the stress fracture? Could it just have been weak? This seemed like an easy explanation—there was scar tissue! It was an old fracture!—and I was angry that the professionals seemed reluctant to tell me it was the likeliest scenario. I wanted to scream, *Do you just not want to say it because you don't want to be wrong, in case he has cancer? Is this because you don't want me to sue you?* I just wanted them to tell me what they really thought was happening. I just wanted them to be honest. Really, I just wanted them to tell me he was going to be okay.

Regardless of the reason, Dr. Pet Daddy told me Peter would need surgery immediately and gave me the names and addresses of a few emergency clinics. It seemed too sudden. I felt like I should research the best surgeons in the city. If we have to do it, there must be a surgeon who is known to be better than the others, and if there is, that is the surgeon Peter should have, right? And shouldn't I get a second opinion?

I called my vet in Brooklyn from Chris's apartment, crying, and told her I didn't know what to do, and to please just tell me what to do. I guess I was hoping that what she would tell me was that I didn't have to do anything, that it was a mistake and that Peter was fine. She, reasonably, seemed unsure about why I felt comfortable crying so much to her on the phone, and explained plainly that she'd gotten the X-rays from "Dr. Pet Daddy," and that Peter needed surgery, now. There were two emergency clinics closer to where I lived; she said they were both good, either would be a good option, it was going to be okay.

I chose one, and Chris drove us to it. A few different veterinarians came to talk to us in the exam room at different points. They explained what would happen; that the surgeon wasn't there today, and that I'd need to leave Peter there overnight so he would be ready for surgery first thing in the morning. But I didn't want to do that. The idea of leaving him there hurt and scared, in this strange building full of injured dogs, terrified me. I did not want him to be alone. I did not want to be alone.

Chris asked if I might be able to bring him home tonight, if there was any reason in terms of care that he should stay there, whether he would lose his place in line for surgery if we took him home, whether it would be okay if I just brought him back early the next morning. They said it would be okay. I could take him home with some pain medicine. The vet was alarmed he hadn't had any yet. "He's very stoic," she said. He was. Chris asked more questions, all the questions you should ask, while I sat with an empty head next to him, holding Peter on my lap, crying and trying not to cry. Is this a break that happens often in dogs? What is the recovery process like? How long will the surgery take? How long will he have to stay at the hospital after the surgery?

The scary thing, as you likely know, was not necessarily that he had a broken elbow but that he would have to go under anesthesia, a vaguely terrifying thing in the abstract and a solidly terrifying thing after you Google it in an exam room. One in two thousand otherwise healthy dogs die from anesthesia-related mishaps, Google told me, adding that it was "fairly rare." Easy for you to say. I signed the forms admitting that I knew he might die, as well as the confusing forms about what sort of lifesaving procedures I did and did not want them to attempt. Why not all of them? I asked. Just because of how much it costs, or are there other reasons? Because if it's how much it costs, I don't care. I'll pay anything. I couldn't get a straight answer, but the woman who brought the forms eventually and reluctantly explained that she hadn't ever seen open-chest cardiopulmonary resuscitation work.

The surgery would cost around seven thousand dollars, they told me. There isn't an amount I wouldn't have put on my credit card, I would pay his surgery off forever if I had to, but I have to admit that amount was fairly breathtaking. It is lucky, though, that the fear of getting into a car accident on the way to Woofstock had forced me to buy pet insurance. I hoped it would cover at least some of the cost. The receptionist assured me that this is exactly what pet insurance was for as she ran my credit card through the terminal.

Back at my apartment, Peter and I sat together on the couch while I tried to sort through the jumble that was my mind. He'd had an injury. Why didn't I notice it before? I wondered if I'd been ignoring it, and if he had been limping. I didn't remember him limping, but he must have been. Right? I wondered if he sustained the injury because of a situation I put him in for the book, or something in my apartment. The agility classes weren't intense, but maybe it was something more ordinary; maybe he got injured jumping on and off my bed. I wondered if he'd been in pain. I wondered if I'd caught it earlier whether I could have gotten him help that didn't require surgery. He was in my care and I had failed him. He was everything to me and I let him get hurt.

How could I not have noticed?

My plan for the next day was to wait in the lobby until Peter was out of surgery. My parents had already planned on coming into the city that day for my brother's birthday—he lives in Manhattan—and they were going to stop by and see me. I wanted to be there, in the building, in case anything happened. I didn't want him to feel like I had left him, if it were at all possible for him to sense that I was still there.

I brought Peter to the clinic early in the morning, gutted with the fear of bringing him to a place from which I might not pick him up. In the lobby I tried to talk to Peter in an uplifting voice. He could sense the location was a bad portent. Oh, it's okay, bunny. They're gonna make you feel better. Oh, you're so good, it's okay puppy. After he was taken away, upstairs, I starting crying in earnest. Luckily the waiting room is dotted, gruesomely, with tissue boxes. I explained to a receptionist—those poor receptionists, dealing with people crying about their dogs every day—that I was going to stay. I had my computer and a book in my backpack. I was just going to sit there and wait. I understood that it was going to be a long time. I was prepared.

She told me to get some water, catch my breath, and go home. I would not be able to see Peter after surgery. They don't let the dogs see their owners because they don't want them to get too excited. I would not be able to talk to the surgeon after surgery; he would call me even if I was sitting in the lobby. There was no reason for me to stay; they would call me with any updates. She spoke gently, and I could tell it was out of kindness, and also a strong desire to not have to spend the entire day watching a grown woman cry.

I felt adrift back at my apartment. I realized I'd never really been there without Peter. When we're out of the apartment, we're out of the apartment together. Padding around, I kept forgetting and remembering.

My parents came by and we sat while I waited for the phone to ring, hyper-aware that every moment that passed could be the moment when something was going wrong. The surgeon was going to call me when Peter was out of surgery, or—also afraid that it might be cancer—if they ran into anything unforeseen, at which point they would talk to me about options before proceeding with anything. It is difficult to decide whether this was a worse day than the one before, but I think this one is the winner.

In the hours after dropping him off I played out his death in my mind. What would I do? I would have to deal with his toys in my apartment. I wouldn't want to get rid of them. I guess I would keep them, but what would I do with his shed hair? I wasn't sure if it would feel worse to keep it or to have it gone. I didn't think I would want to be in our apartment at all. I couldn't be there alone. I would have to move out. I guess I could move home, I thought. I don't think I would want to write anymore. Maybe I would get a real job. I certainly wasn't going to write a sad book about my sad dead dog. The world didn't need that.

It struck me that I would have to tell people. I contemplated a dead-dog phone tree where I could just tell someone to spread the word. I would eventually have to see other people's living dogs and pretend I didn't resent them, and how was I going to do that? How could I be around Chris and Frank? My phone was full of images of him, that would have to go too. Maybe it had been wrong to make this fragile little creature the center of my entire world.

I hadn't heard from the hospital before it was time for my parents to meet my brother at a restaurant in the Meatpacking District. Showing great restraint, I'd only called twice to check in. I didn't want to be alone at home, waiting, and decided to go with my family, and upon arriving at the restaurant requested that the hostess seat us wherever had the best cell reception. (She was very understanding of this request even before we explained it was for dog surgical reasons.) Not long after arriving I got a call and ran outside, and my dad followed me. I answered the phone, "IS HE OKAY?" The surgeon laughed. He was okay. Everything went fine.

They didn't see any sign of cancer during the surgery, but did a blood test that would be some extra sum of money. The surgeon explained that Peter would almost certainly have arthritis, which seemed to me like a silly thing to bring up. He was alive. He did not die. He was alive and I could pick him up in the morning. I still had him. I could keep his shed hair, I could keep his toys, I could keep our apartment,

I could keep our life. Back at the table, I downed my cocktail and ordered another.

While I waited for him in the lobby the next morning I watched a woman attempt to coax her dog away from the door, where he was desperately trying to leave. "We're not going, monkey. Monkey, we have to stay here," she said cheerily, through tears.

I was so preoccupied with the fact that Peter hadn't died, I'd forgotten to think about the fact that he would be in a cone, and that they would have to shave an entire quadrant of his body for the surgery. He was brought down to the waiting room and I was at once so relieved and completely gutted. He was so delicate, with a large cone and a fresh scar. His skin on the injured leg, which was now fitted with several screws, was bare. The surgeon explained a cast could lead to an infection.

At home, we watched TV and cuddled together in a pile of pillows and blankets on the floor. I made him chicken and gave him treats. We slept in my bed at night, but for the next week we mostly spent our days in the floor pillow pile. He was on a pill-taking schedule that got us up at 4:00 a.m. and then 6:00 a.m., at which point I would beg him with increasing desperation to please, please, please take his medicine. He was incredible at sniffing it out. He laughed at a pill pocket, rolled his eyes at peanut butter. Different food items in the house might mask the pills once, but he never let it happen with the same food item twice. It was as President George W.

Bush once said: "Fool me once, shame on...shame on you. Fool me...you can't get fooled again."

The cancer test came back negative. The mystery of why this happened lingers, but if that was going to be the definitive answer, I'd rather have the question. He eventually got stronger, less sleepy, more accustomed to his cone and body. (I bought him a softer cone online, which he appreciated.) Over the next month I carried him everywhere. The elevator in our building usually works, so there are only a few sets of steps between us and outside. There I would carry him to different dirt patches, praying that he would go, and usually, eventually, he would. I would see other dogs walking freely and think, *You jerks*. I was sad for Peter's loss, unable to run or play. It got easier after a while. He started being able to walk a little, hopping on one front leg, and then eventually getting the other one into the mix. After a one-month checkup, our surgeon said he was doing well, but that he needed to be restricted for another month. That was okay. We didn't need to do much, anyway.

We headed to our two-month checkup on a clear, sunny day, and I was nervous but ready to hear good news. I think this is what did it. I did not have the appropriate amount of fear; the somber dread that karmically protects against bad news. His elbow was not healing. "It's a really tough area," the surgeon said. He might have a permanent limp, but before succumbing to that possibility he wanted to try one more thing—a splint. I asked him to explain exactly what this meant—for how long? Would it hurt him? Would I ever take it off? It would stay on for five weeks, and cover half of his leg. I'd come back for checkups just about every week to make sure it wasn't causing him any pain. "He's tough," he said. "He won't show you."

After everything, I just wasn't really prepared for this. It was time for him to have his old life back. Time for him to be able to run and play, and walk farther than the block around our apartment. My sweet Peter is not particularly antsy indoors, but it's not what brings him the uninhibited kind of wild joy that, selfishly, makes you feel like you're doing a good job as his caretaker. He likes to run around, he likes to sniff all sorts of different pee. I have to imagine the pee around our apartment building got old after a while.

When they brought him back to me the splint was covered in gauze, and it took up about half of his body. He walked like a stuffed animal that had only managed to come three-quarters of the way to life. He looked much worse than he had before.

As the vet bills racked up, I was more grateful than ever for my paranoid pre-Woofstock buying of pet insurance. It covered almost all of it. And the cast, at least, made it obvious why I was carrying him. "Oh, that's why you're always carrying him!" three neighbors—genuinely, three—said to me the first time I took him out with his new horrifying accoutrements. Peter hated it. I hated it. Imagine thinking you're okay, thinking you're on the mend, and then you're put in a huge fucking cast and no one can even tell you why. He couldn't sleep. He couldn't get comfortable. It was painful to watch him try to lie down, difficult to watch him try to walk. I worried that he was in pain under the cast, or itchy. I had to take him back for regular bandage changes, because the gauze would shrink, and the plastic would poke into his skin. Between changes I stuffed socks underneath. I so badly wanted to help him. And I badly wanted it to be me instead.

My neighbors are very sweet, but for the five weeks Peter was in his cast I couldn't go outside without talking to more than one of them about his injury. His tiny turtle body was pathetically cute, I admit, and it couldn't help but draw attention. The issue was not that everyone cared, it was genuinely sweet, but that I had to explain, over and over, *what happened*. And the question "what happened," about a tiny creature wholly within your care, only feels like: What did you let happen? What did you do that caused this, how were you neglectful? *What did I let happen?*

I would explain that he was running and it broke; that it had been weak from a fracture. They would make a pained face. It put me in the uncomfortable position of comforting them, saying it's okay, he's healing, he's on the mend—at once making me feel like a liar for attempting a sunny outlook, and heartless for not mirroring their pain. I'm not sure what I should have done.

In the last week he spent with his cast, I finally expressed how I truly felt to an unsuspecting woman who stopped me to ask about him while walking her dog—that I felt horrible, that I wished I could take it away or just do something. "You're doing something," she said. "You're carrying him."

When the five weeks were up, I took him back to the vet, actually happy to be there for the second time. I had to drop him off again, so the surgeon could spend some time doing physical therapy with him before releasing him back to me, but leaving him wasn't as hard this time. When I finally saw him without his cast, I cried. His body was there. I could itch it for him, if it was itchy. He could even itch it himself. The surgeon told me the bone had healed more—still maybe not enough to prevent him from retaining a small limp, but the cast had at least been somewhat successful. I was just glad it was gone.

The next morning we woke up in my bed and he was there, his whole body, in the final phase of healing. I felt like I'd unclenched a muscle I hadn't realized I was clenching, relieved of pain that had been present in my body for so long I'd lost awareness of it. It was just such a fucking relief.

I'm not sure we'll ever return to dance. (Do you remember that we started this with dance?) It seems like the universe would prefer we stay away, and I can accept that. But we'll still spin and twist alone together, at home. I'm still going to attempt to get him to walk under my leg. And I still love his sunny, funny face.

Chapter 13

WILL MY DOG
GO TO HEAVEN?

Certain questions hovered over my Catholic upbringing, like the Holy Ghost on so many felt Pentecost banners. Do I have to go to church, and can I please stay home? Will you go to hell for chewing on the host? Did my fourth-grade substitute teacher think getting ashes on my forehead would actually cure my migraine, and was she ashamed when I instead vomited on my desk? And of course, will my dog go to heaven?

Despite attending Catholic school from first through twelfth grade, the answers to most of these questions never presented themselves. Then, in 2014, it seemed like one might. Suddenly, on a December day as unremarkable as any other, Pope Francis was reported as saying that dogs (*dogs!*) were allowed (*allowed!*) into heaven (*heaven!*), which is in fact something he did not say.

—Or is it?

It is not. It's actually sort of confusing, but if you say ten "Hail Mary"s I will attempt to explain it to you. Just kidding. I will explain it to you for free, as an act of charity.

As you may know, Pope Francis was deemed a "Cool Pope" early in his papal career. The distinction has faded a bit after dustups like when he compared aborting fetuses discovered to have birth defects through prenatal testing to Nazi eugenics programs, and when he said only heterosexual couples should have children. Those things were not very cool. But, as they say, you either make the (surprisingly long) Wikipedia list of "popes who died violently" as a Cool Pope, or you live long enough to become much less cool than people originally thought you were because of how you once blessed an Italian porn star's parrot.

But Pope Francis's "Cool Pope" distinction was still going strong when he either did or did not say dogs could go to heaven in 2014, either going or not going against conservative interpretations of the Catholic Church's doctrine regarding whether animals in general have immortal souls. (You need a soul to get into heaven.) The account that went around first was spread so widely, and made such an impact, that none of the Catholic scholars I spoke to for what you're reading, nor any member of my large Irish Catholic family, nor any of the non-Catholic co-workers I asked (people who make their living following and reporting news) even recalled that it had been misreported and eventually corrected. All anyone remembered was that Pope Francis said dogs were allowed into heaven. The original story went like this: The pope met a little boy who was distraught over the recent death of his dog. To comfort him, the pope said: "One day, we will see our animals again in the eternity of Christ. Paradise is open to all of God's creatures."

"Pope Francis Says Dogs Can Go to Heaven," said *TIME*. "Dogs in Heaven? Pope Francis Leaves Pearly Gates Open," said the *New York Times*. "Pope: Dogs Can Go to Heaven," said CNN. "All Dogs Go to Heaven! Pope Francis Confirms Paradise Is Open to All of God's Creatures," said E! Yes, who is or is not allowed in heaven hadn't been so hotly discussed since season two, episode nine of *The Sopranos*, when "Christopha" briefly dies and says he saw Brendan and Mikey in hell and they told him to tell Tony and Paulie "three o'clock."

That animals could go to heaven and thus have a soul would have had repercussions beyond altering the image many seem to hold of a strictly dogless afterlife. It would mean treating animals poorly was against God's word; it would, of course, mean eating them was a sin.

But it turns out none of that stuff with the boy actually happened. Or at least, none of it happened with Pope Francis. Instead of consoling a child, Pope Francis spoke in a general audience at the Vatican. And instead of saying in fairly clear terms that we would see our beloved animals again in the afterlife, he said, according to Vatican Radio, "The Holy Scripture teaches us that the fulfillment of this wonderful design also affects everything around us." Uh-*huh*. "Media Widely Misreports That Pope Francis Says Dogs Can Go to Heaven," read an updated *Today* headline.

The confusion came when the Italian newspaper *Corriere della Sera* interpreted the remarks to be more dog-specific than they were perhaps intended, and compared them to a quote from Pope Paul VI, who died in 1978. That quote was, in fact, "One day, we will see our animals again in the eternity of Christ. Paradise is open to all of God's creatures." And it was, in fact, delivered while consoling a boy who had recently lost his dog. Clearly, whether or not animals are allowed into heaven is not a new topic of discussion.

According to a Reuters report, *Corriere della Sera* gave their story the rather easy-to-misinterpret headline, "The Pope and Animals. 'Paradise Is Open to All Creatures.'" The Italian leg of the *Huffington Post* picked the article up, attributed the quote and story to St. Paul (rather than Pope Paul VI), and reported that Pope Francis delivered the line while quoting St. Paul. Through a game of heavenly telephone, the nuance drifted farther and farther away, and Pope Francis eventually came to say that dogs were allowed into heaven.

There are a few obvious reasons why the story spread so wildly. As someone who's worked in online media for a decade, I can tell you that a new, clear announcement from the Catholic Church's highest (and, at that point, *coolest*) authority saying that dogs are now officially allowed into heaven—spoken to a young boy whose dog had died, no less—translates to guaranteed clicks, particularly from an audience who had no idea that popes have apparently been saying this kind of thing for a while. You don't want to fact-check it; it's too good, too sharable, too much in line with the already-set narrative of the rule-breaking Pope Francis, an almost meme-like internet figure known well by even non-Catholics. And it's all of those things because it's what people want. Not the aggrieved Catholics, already upset with Francis's apparent totally-chill-man attitude, using it as further proof that he needed reining in. But to everyone else. Most people. Even if we don't believe in heaven, we want it for our dogs. They deserve to go to "heaven."

But—a pope did say that, though. About paradise being open to all of God's creatures. Not the internet-famous pope, but still, a pope. And what Pope Francis said, "The Holy Scripture teaches us that the fulfillment of this wonderful design also affects everything around us"—still seems to suggest that, if fulfillment is entering the kingdom of heaven, everything around us will...do it. Yes?

Pope Francis seemed to follow up his comments in a 2015 encyclical (a papal letter sent to all the Catholic bishops) titled "Praise Be." Most of the letter focused on climate change, but it also dealt directly with the way we treat animals. "We must forcefully reject the notion that our being created in God's image and given dominion over the earth justifies absolute domination over other creatures," he wrote. "The Bible has no place for a tyrannical anthropocentrism." And yes, I am also always saying this.

"Pope Benedict XVI, whose papacy began in 2005 and ended in 2013, was actually the person that really got it going," Charles Camosy told me. Camosy is a professor of theological and social ethics at Fordham University. "He was well known as an animal lover—he had to be told he couldn't invite stray cats into the Vatican. He explicitly said that the way we treat animals in factory farms is not biblical. It's not the way God intended us to interact with animals."

And even before Pope Benedict XVI, Pope John Paul II (head of the church from 1978 to 2005) said "animals possess a soul and men must love and feel solidarity with our smaller brethren." He added that they are "as near to God as men are." Huh.

It seems to me like dogs have been getting into heaven for a while.

Harry Attridge, a New Testament scholar and Sterling Professor of Divinity at Yale University, disagrees. He does not believe that they are up there chewing on heaven bones, barking at God, running around off-leash at all times, and performing canine freestyle with the angels. "In a strict Aristotelian sense you can say, yeah, an animal has a soul. But that doesn't make it the same kind of soul that a human being has, in the Christian theological context."

"For most of the church's history there's been a sense that dogs have this animal soul," Camosy said, "but it's not the kind that goes to heaven. Parallel with that thought is that animals have always been thought of as being part of the afterlife."

He cited Isaiah 11:6, which talks about what the end of the world and beginning of the new world will look like (do not read on if you'd like to keep it a surprise). "The wolf will live with the lamb, the leopard will lie down with the goat, the calf and the lion and the yearling together; and a little child will lead them." That sounds like animals to me.

Both Camosy and Attridge pointed me to the Catechism of the Catholic Church, which is essentially the guidebook for the Catholic faith. It says, in essence, to not be an asshole. "Animals are God's creatures. He surrounds them with his providential care. By their mere existence they bless him and give him glory. Thus men owe them kindness."

It also says, in essence, that we are allowed to use animals for our means: "God entrusted animals to the stewardship of those whom he created in his own image. Hence it is legitimate to use animals for food and clothing."

Camosy said he hoped the Catholic Church would wrestle with these opposing viewpoints. "Jesus had very clear things to say about violence and war. There's an ongoing debate between pacifists and just war theorists. I think we're in a similar situation with violence toward animals and how we think about animals."

But does Camosy think dogs go to heaven? "Yes. There's absolutely no question. There's no question."

Does Attridge? "I don't think so, no."

It's difficult.

To me, it just doesn't make sense that dogs and other animals wouldn't be allowed into heaven. Though I understand the reluctance to accept it. It's kind of like believing in ghosts—a domino effect of beliefs has to follow. Souls, planes, an afterlife, someone always watching you do your weird little routines, and also when you're nude. If animals were allowed into heaven, what would that mean for how we treat them on earth? Would we have to stop packing chickens into cages? Would we baptize rabbits? Could we still eat hamburgers? It's extra tough because the Catholic Church is famous for an absence of contradiction in its stated and lived beliefs.

I don't think it particularly matters whether or not you believe in heaven. (I personally didn't until I saw that *Sopranos* episode; now I'm not so sure.) That it exists as an idea is enough. It's more than just the principle of it—it's the hope and the possibility, the possible relief of a little bit of sadness. But it's also *just the principle of it!* Why shouldn't dogs be allowed in heaven, if it exists? Heaven makes sense more as a place for dogs than it does as a place for humans. Humans are awful. They're cruel and selfish and abusive and unworthy, and dogs, all animals, are just stuck here with them. Humans destroy the earth, disappear species, dress their dog in a costume and put them in a little purse, and then the human gets a chance to go to heaven and the animals—what?

Peter is going to die. And he's going to die, in the grand scheme of all things, pretty soon. Because he was picked up as a stray, I'm not even really sure how old he is. I doubt adopting a puppy is much easier. The more you love them—the more attached you get, the more times they come and sit right on top of you when you're sad, the more times they react to your arrival home as the most exciting thing that has ever happened to them—the sharper it gets. How many more winters? How many more summers? How many more times will you be able to make them their own dog-friendly birthday cake? Ten? Five? Three?

In more well-adjusted moments I guess there's sort of a beauty in it. You're lucky enough to have an ephemeral piece of light as a part of your life, aware of its impermanence from the beginning and loving it wholly anyway. Knowing someone who is only good, and getting to be their caretaker. Letting this dog believe that you are the sun and the moon, even though you are just a human. Protecting them until you no longer can.

They are good and they are everything, and fuck you. Fuck you for saying my dog isn't going to be allowed into "heaven"!

Chapter 14

MY DOG

Here is what I know about Peter.

I know that any time I leave a room he assumes it's because I've gone to get him a treat. I come back to find him sitting, relaxed and upright, patiently waiting, ready to receive whatever I've brought for him—anything's fine, he's not picky. "Here I am," his eyes say. "I've been waiting, and I'm ready for what you've come to surprise me with." He's effectively taught me to, now, yes, bring him a treat upon my return any time I leave a room. He is excellent at this trick and has also taught me to give him a treat any time we come inside from a walk. We come in, I unleash him, and he sits, big eyes staring up at me. I sigh. "Okay, let me get your treat."

He doesn't like blueberries. He'll beg me for a blueberry whenever I have them as if he is desperate for it, *please, my god, give me a blueberry or any sustenance at all*, and, though I try to explain to him that he absolutely does not like blueberries, and in fact dislikes them so much that he seems to not even understand how to eat them, letting them fall from his mouth to the floor as if he's suddenly forgotten how to masticate, he does not relent in begging, so I give him one. He lets it fall from his mouth. What a horrible trick I've pulled . . . to give him this trash?

He also doesn't it like when I use his butt as a pillow. Sometimes he'll lie in such a way that his head is on my leg, and his big butt is right by my head. Very tempting. He'll allow me to rest on it for a few minutes before he groans and repositions, annoyed to have to move when he knows I know he doesn't like having his butt used for non-butt purposes. Well. Don't have such a tempting butt, then.

He's afraid of cats. He doesn't want you to know this, but it's true. If you encounter a cat with him he'll lead you away from a cat with a ferocity that suggests he is merely protecting you from the cat, in case maybe you're the one who is afraid. But between you and me that's not the case; it's because he is the one who is afraid. It's nothing to be ashamed of, but try telling him that.

He hates getting his teeth brushed, but appreciates when the job has been done. After I put away the toothbrush and chicken toothpaste, he cuddles up, almost apologetic. I think he likes having a clean mouth. I understand the process is difficult, though, and I don't blame him for giving me, oh my god, the hardest fucking time about it.

I love learning new things about Peter. It is, I would say, my primary source of happiness. I love to observe him moving around my apartment, sniffing, making a decision about what he wants to do. I love looking at his face really close up. The hair around his mouth, his tiny nose, his large whiskers, his puppy eyes. I love when he has his snout rested on his paws and lifts up his face and his skin has been molded into a snarl, and you can see a little bit of tooth. I love when he pounces in excitement, like a red panda, when he hears the word "play." I love holding him back from dinner with the "wait" command, waiiiit, for an unreasonable amount of time, revving him up, so he launches his body like a racehorse hearing a gunshot when he gets the "okay!"

As his sole caretaker I feel like I've been entrusted not only with keeping him alive and fed and safe, but also with the job of figuring out who he is; knowing it and remembering it, telling anyone who will listen. "He actually likes carrots, he's only not eating them now because you gave him cheese first and he knows there's a better option." Watching him, attempting to remember his patterns, trying to figure him out.

The rest of us get to have lives full of friends and loved ones and all of these people who get to really know us, or at least attempt to, but our dogs pretty much only have us. Sure they know our neighbors, and friends, and cousins, and their agility classmates, and they know whichever psychics you've introduced them to, and of course they're beloved by all of them. But you can't really know a dog casually. The world of people who have the opportunity to really get to know who they are is a fairly small one. It's just us. If we don't attempt to know them, they won't be known. And they should be known.

Right now, I'm sitting on the ground and Peter sitting beside me, looking at me like he needs something. His left ear is flopped over and his right is alert, which is their usual position. He's just had his dinner, so what he wants now is to play. After I finish with this, I'll take his duck (the platypus), yell "THAT'S MY DUCK!," and move it around his feet while he pounces and attempts to grab it with his mouth, but not forcefully enough that he actually gets it and ruins the game. We'll play for a bit, until he gets sick of it. After that I'm not sure what he'll want to do. We'll see.

ACKNOWLEDGMENTS

This is, of course, all because of Peter. He is my driving force, my primary source of joy. It's somewhat surprising to me that having him in my life never, even for a second, stops feeling incredibly special. It never gets old, and every day I am newly grateful. As I'm typing this right now, he's sticking his sweet little snout under my hand, and I assume this is because he can sense that I haven't written anything funny yet. I do apologize for that. But I am wildly lucky for many reasons, and he's a big one. There are some humans I should thank, too.

This book wouldn't exist if my friend Leah Finnegan hadn't encouraged me to write about DNA testing Peter for the Outline, which I admittedly only did so I could expense the DNA test. She is a brilliant editor and a wonderful friend, and I am grateful she lets me hang out with her even though she is much smarter and cooler than I am.

My agent, Tina Pohlman, would not let me not write this book. I was terrified and lazy and insecure, but she just would not stop bothering me about it, and I appreciate that more than I can express. I want to thank her, also, for telling me how to write a book. I had absolutely no idea.

And speaking of, thank you to Maddie Caldwell, the book's editor, for saving me from producing a book much, much worse than the one you have today. If you still think it's bad, well. The fault is Maddie's. And thank you to the rest of the team at Grand Central. I really can't overstate how little I knew about this process before entering into it, but everyone there was wonderful and patient and made it seem less completely daunting.

Alex Balk was the first person to encourage me to write a book about Peter. I think the suggestion was somewhat cynical and based mostly on his assumption that people who like dogs will buy anything dog-related, but I appreciate the encouragement nonetheless, and, of course, I do hope he was right.

I want to thank Jesse David Fox for a lot of things—reading embarrassing drafts, tirelessly listening to me worry out loud, bringing me to fancy events when Alina can't go—but mostly for being my friend.

Chris Wendelken and Frank Wendelken, thank you for caring about me and supporting me and putting up with me. I assume I was not particularly pleasant to be around during the more stressful parts of the book-writing process, but you did not abandon me, and you kept me sane, and I am so grateful.

Acknowledgments

Thank you to Therisa Ingley and the Sweet Onion Animal Protection Society, and everyone at Badass Brooklyn, and everyone at Sean Casey Animal Rescue, and everyone else who works to rescue and home dogs. The work you do is difficult and important and life-changing. Truly, thank you. And thank you to all of my sources for letting me ask you profoundly dumb questions, and for answering them so kindly and patiently.

And some others before I go. Thank you to my mom and dad, my brothers Patrick and Thomas, Grandma and Papa Conaboy, Grandma and Papa Kennedy, all of my aunts and uncles and cousins, of which there are five million, and my friends Jordan Sargent, William Turton, Allie Jones, Silvia Killingsworth, Mike Dang, Megan Reynolds, Dusty Matthews, Michael Macher, Jen Gann, Katie Heaney, and James Hamblin. I tried not to talk to you all about the book too much, but I definitely did talk about it too much. So, thank you.

ABOUT THE AUTHOR

KELLY CONABOY is a writer in Brooklyn, New York. She's written for *New York Magazine*'s The Cut, as well as the Hairpin, Gawker, and Videogum. Most of those websites no longer exist. (This is not because of Kelly.) She's been published by *The Atlantic*, the *New Yorker*, and the *New York Times*. Her humor piece for the *New Yorker*'s "Shouts & Murmurs" section was adapted for the New Yorker Radio Hour and read for air by Ellie Kemper.